UNFORTUNATE ENDS

Unfortunate ENDS

On *Murder* and *Misadventure* in *Medieval* England

• SØREN LILY •

unbound

First published in 2022

Unbound
Level 1, Devonshire House, One Mayfair Place, London W1J 8AJ
www.unbound.com

Text design by PDQ Digital Media Solutions Ltd.

A CIP record for this book is available from the British Library

ISBN 978-1-80018-136-6 (hardback)
ISBN 978-1-80018-137-3 (ebook)

Printed in Great Britain by CPI Group (UK)

1 3 5 7 9 8 6 4 2

UNFORTUNATE ENDS

CONTENTS

Unfortunate Ends

A Necessary Introduction by the Author

It was sometime around 2010 that I became aware of the existence of medieval coroners' rolls; I got my hands on a copy of Barbara Hanawalt's *The Ties That Bound*, which takes a look at daily life in the late Middle Ages through reports of accidental deaths. Not to be sated solely by second-hand accounts of these rolls, I sought them out online and found a handful of them, which I pored over, thoroughly delighted to be able to come face to face with the past in such a way, no matter how grim.

There was something oddly funny about it all. I have a macabre sense of humour, which may not come as a surprise, and I was struck by the absurdity of people endlessly dying in ditches, being murdered by mysterious clerks and drowning in mill-ponds. Causes of death began to function almost as a punchline, or as recurring characters, haunting a medieval landscape, causing horrendous mayhem despite their mundanity. Oddly enough, these deaths brought the Middle Ages to life, giving me glimpses of who hung out where after work, of what games they played, of where children wandered, and even provided a wealth of information on common names and naming conventions of the era like nothing I had really seen before. Through their deaths, they brought the people of the Middle Ages so close – thousands of Rogers, Williams, Henrys and Gregs, handfuls of Alices, Margereys and Isabels, and not a single thing that sounded like it had been barfed out of a medieval historical novel.* Moreover, every other person, especially in the Oxford rolls, seemed to be a clerk – whatever that was. The more I read, the more I wanted to share these deaths with the wider world, to make them accessible to those that wouldn't likely know to seek them out. How amazing and precious the past can be, but how obscure and hard to grasp!

I must admit, my first instinct was to somehow try to work these deaths into a comic. It was a very bad idea, and I am not much of a comic writer anyway. So the comic was thankfully scrapped after the first attempt. But I had been on Twitter for a few years, and Twitter bots were fairly popular and plausible to make, so I spent a few weekends over a month or two transcribing a few hundred tweets from four different collections of coroners' rolls. These were some long, brain-bending sessions, taking paragraphs of nineteenth-century translations of medieval Latin, with all their run-on sentences, and trying to sum them up succinctly in just one tiny 140-characters-or-fewer tweet. That's why the syntax got a little wonky sometimes. But it

---

* The only one I've found that does is a man named Drogo Prior, who died in Deerhurst in Gloucestershire in 1392. He was killed on Christmas Eve by one of his own servants.

was only a small project anyway, and, I figured, not one that very many people would be interested in...

I set my weird little tweets up in a bot, to tweet randomly from a cache every twelve hours or so, and thus the Medieval Death Bot was born.

My instinct to share these deaths proved to be a good one, as the bot eventually garnered followers in the hundreds of thousands. Which I still can't believe. Sometime in 2018 I was approached to write this book, based on a handful of deaths that appear on the bot. Now, long after I promised the book would be done (please forgive me, I had no idea how long non-fiction takes to write), we have *Unfortunate Ends*. It's been an extreme labour of love, one I've worked through while juggling my handful of side-hustles that amount to some sort of livelihood, as well as long bouts of carpal tunnel and, towards the very end, a global pandemic. But all the late nights digging around these old rolls, falling down deep rabbit holes about the shifting street names of London, and scouring every footnote and bibliography of my medieval library for new leads, has been an immense pleasure.

To everyone who helped make this book possible, and waited so patiently for me to finish it, I thank you. You've helped me – just some guy with an inexplicable love for a time long ago – write something that I hope will be both an entertaining and illuminating look at the Middle Ages.

In reading this book, you may wonder why so many of

these deaths are violent accidents or murders. It can create quite a frightening image of the past, leaving you wondering if anyone ever died of old age. Well – they certainly did! But these were not deaths that required a visit from the coroner. Like modern coroners, medieval coroners only examined accidental deaths ('death by misadventure'), sudden deaths (which could include accidents, but also included homicide, murder and suicide) and deaths in prisons. The latter is the single exception to seeing 'died of old age' as a cause of death. If someone died what was known as a 'good death', having had their last rites and all their chattels divided amongst their heirs, the services of the coroner were not needed.

The coroner himself was usually a knight (though after the fourteenth century it seems he was only required to be a landowner), elected in county courts to serve locally. Each county had four coroners, and each coroner had their own clerk, whose job it was to write the inquest reports, though they sometimes also conducted inquests on their own. The office of coroner was a job kept ideally for life, though that was on the condition of 'good behaviour', and it wasn't uncommon for new coroners to be elected once a new king took the throne. While one of the perks was being exempt from having to appear on a jury, it seems not to have had many other benefits, and was so undesirable a position that some sought royal grants to be exempt from ever being burdened with the role.

The main function of the coroner was twofold: to thoroughly review the cause of death to ensure that any guilty parties involved would go to trial, and to collect fees for the king. For the coroner served the king foremost; while he was elected by the county itself, his loyalties were intended to lie with the king, and it was his responsibility to see that all the fees were gathered for the exchequer. While some boroughs elected their own coroners with permission from the king, manors were not usually allowed them, given the fear that the coroner would be more loyal to his lord than to the king.

Inquest reports give us a good idea of what happened in cases of sudden death. If the death had been witnessed, and the person had been 'feloniously slain', the person who witnessed it was required to 'raise the hue and cry'. This simply meant that if you saw some shit going down – robbery, murder, assault – you had a legal obligation to start hooting and hollering about it. Neighbours and bystanders who heard this were required to come and help apprehend the offender – if they could be caught. The chase of a criminal could be relentless, spanning as many counties as necessary, until they were delivered to a sheriff for justice. Most times in the cases of felonious slayings, the murderer fled, and either sought sanctuary, or was never heard of again. Raising the hue was not required if a crime was not suspected, but it was still common practice to alert the neighbours, who could then notify the bailiff, who would send for the coroner. In some cases, such as that of Agnes Perone, the coroner showed up the very same afternoon, but it seems that sometimes he could take up to two days to arrive on the scene for the necessary inquest.

Two juries were summoned to appear at the inquest. The coroner's jury, known as the 'villatae jury', varied in number from county to county, but usually consisted of a handful of men – traditionally the reeve and four others (though sometimes anywhere between three and eight) – from four neighbouring vills (a township or village). Twelve other men, presumably from the township in which the death had occurred, also appeared to pass verdicts. The coroner's inquest, however, was only a preliminary inquiry to ascertain the possible guilt of any involved parties. The actual trial of any guilty parties would take place later, and it was at this trial that these same juries would appear again to aid in passing a verdict.

With the juries secured and in attendance, the scene of the death was described by those who had witnessed it. Some clerks go to great length to describe it as vividly as possible, with every twist and turn and clarifying relation ('Matilda, wife of John Atwell') repeated ad nauseam, but some are quite succinct, giving the death the barest and briefest description. This is either the result of personal preference, or it could be that the witnesses and pledges themselves didn't offer much information. *Yes, John killed so and so out in the field. We heard it. They were fighting about cows. Let's move on and get all this over with, I've got shit to do.*

If the deceased had survived some time after their accident or attack, it is noted, as well as usually whether or not they were able to receive their last rites or not. We get some truly grisly glimpses here of what the human body can endure, such as people shot with arrows living another entire month before they finally died. And alongside the grisly is the odd; women who were involved in accidents while pregnant, for example, and then later died in childbirth. Due to their involvement in an accident, their death is still investigated.

With any possible guilt, or the clarification of an accident, out of the way, next came the juicy part – figuring out who owed what to the king because someone had died!

In cases of misadventure we encounter one of the most baffling and frequently asked-about aspects of these inquests: deodands. Many descriptions of deaths in the rolls have the curious trait of mentioning the prices of items involved in deaths – a knife worth a penny, a pan worth sixpence, malt worth ten shillings – but why in the world would this need to be stated? What possible help could this be to the dead, or those they left behind?

These items with listed prices are known as 'deodands'. In short, a deodand was an item that was believed to have caused, or had aided in, an accidental death. This item was appraised in value, which became a fee that had to be paid to the crown at the eyre (a circulating court). When Richard le Brewere died in 1300, having fallen down the stairs while carrying a bag of malt, the step of the stair itself was considered the fateful piece in this scene, and given a value of 2s. That step is a deodand.

The origins of the deodand are obscure, but the idea behind them – that there is an item involved in accidental death that must be somehow surrendered or otherwise 'cleansed' – is not. Anglo-Saxon law, cemented in the Laws of Alfred the Great (circa AD 900), practised 'noxal surrender', in which the instrument of death (in cases of accidents) was forfeit to the victim's family by the wrongdoer. This was not intended to be a complete and whole compensation to the victim's family for the loss, but was given to ensure no further legal action was taken, and that the wrongdoer did not *have* to provide full compensation. While noxal surrender did not evolve into deodand, there is an oddly similar sentiment behind the idea that there is a single item connected to the death that must be dealt with in some way. Of course, while it seems like it would make more sense (or at least be more charitable) to have the wrongdoer give the deodand fee to the victim's family, the royal exchequer instead put it in the king's pocket.

This might shine some small light on the term itself, which comes from the Latin *deo dandum*, 'to be given to God'. This has led many to erroneously believe that once the crown had the deodand, it would put the money towards some charitable or holy purpose. However, there is no evidence of this happening. The best guess at the origin of the word, at the idea that this fee was something given over to God, is that the king represented holy justice on earth, and was able to receive funds accordingly.[*]

All of which is to say, if you died in a boat worth 4s. 6d. someone (in most cases it was the sheriff) had to cough up 4s. 6d. to send to the king's treasury. Why? Well, because there was money to be made in death. And deodand certainly wasn't the only way.

When it came to felonious slayings, the king received the chattels of the wrongdoers, which were named and ascertained in the coroner's inquest, but not given over until the trial at the eyre. Chattels included goods, animals, houses and land (but not women, by popular misconception). Laws surrounding forfeiture of chattels by the offending party changed through the high Middle Ages, seeming to start off with a blanket requirement of forfeiture even in cases of accidental homicide, and later allowing certain pardons in cases of what we would now call manslaughter, or of self-defence.

The fees do not end here, however. There is one final, somewhat unlikely fine documented in the thirteenth-century rolls from Bedfordshire, and it is the tradition of *presenting Englishry*. When the Normans invaded and took over England in 1066, they created a law that any Englishman who killed

---

[*] An exception to this, it seems, is that small deodand fees may have gone to clerks in certain shires. In Kent in the years 1313 and 1314, there is mention of clerks (presumably the coroner's clerk, who may have conducted the inquest himself in place of the coroner) receiving deodands if they did not exceed sixpence halfpenny. Why this is, though, I'm not sure.

a Norman was to be fined for it. And so in cases of sudden death, evidence had to be given that the victim was, in fact, an Englishman, and not a Norman. But as time went on and the English and Normans intermarried, the distinction between Norman and English ceased to be quite so prominent, making it hard to implement. Its scarce presence in the Bedfordshire rolls indicates that the practice had died out long before it was officially abolished in the fourteenth century.

All these fees, and who will 'see to them', are listed at the end of the inquest report, and that sums up the entire affair. Most reports average about two paragraphs, half of that being the long-winded explanation of the date (which you will get a good look at in the first chapter) and the vills from whence the villatae jury was gathered.

This book uses four main sources for its deaths: *Calendar of Coroners Rolls of the City of London A.D. 1300–1378*, edited by Reginald R. Sharpe; *Select Cases from the Coroners' Rolls A.D. 1265–1413*, edited by Charles Gross; *Records of Mediæval Oxford*, edited by H. E. Salter; and *Records of the Borough of Leicester*, edited by Mary Bateson, all of which can be found freely on Archive.org. While many more coroners' rolls exist, they are not easily accessible, especially to someone in the US who does not read medieval Latin. Thankfully, these books were translated, edited and compiled in the late nineteenth and early twentieth centuries, and digitised in the early twenty-first. Due to their translation, they do not represent an authentic medieval vocabulary as it would have been used at the time, nor do they represent what would have been spoken,[*] especially since their translation into Victorian English is to account for some slight anachronisms in terms, such as the word 'highwayman'.

The only thing missing from this book is the presence of drowning deaths which, while occurring frequently, do not offer much in the way of mystery. Medieval people, by and large, did not know how to swim, and whether they were disrobing to bathe in mill-ponds or attempting to navigate their way home while drunk and falling into ditches, bodies of open water proved a challenge. Deceptive currents in rivers especially can be blamed for many deaths occurring from attempting to bathe, or while bathing. Drainage ditches littered the medieval world in order to control rain flow away from the roads. These were often crossed with timber which allowed people to walk over them safely... or not so safely, as the coroners' rolls let us know.

Here I hope to offer a full buffet of deaths for varying diets, with sweets served alongside savouries in true medieval fashion. A few of them were specifically requested by and illustrated for those who backed the book at the highest tier, while the rest were picked for their insights into everyday medieval life. There has always been something inspiring and

---

[*] The nobility would have been speaking Anglo-Norman up until about the mid-fourteenth century, with everyone else speaking Middle English.

comforting to me in studying the common people of the past – it speaks to both the fortitude of humanity to survive any hardship and the enduring commonality we have as human beings. Our medieval forebears may have dressed, spoken and lived quite differently, but deep down, we have always been pretty much the same.

1

THE INNOCENT CLERK

The Death of Roger de Metham

from *Records of Medieval Oxford*

or our first foray into the world of medieval death, we must discuss the death of a clerk. These medieval men have been thrust into unintentional infamy by the bot on Twitter, clogging the streets of Oxford with their drunken altercations, their maiming and murdering, and their endless squabbles over football that end with their brains being spewed out from halberd-hacked skulls.

These accounts create a frightening image of the English Middle Ages and who inhabited them, but who were these clerks really? What were they all doing in Oxford? And just why were they so violent? Looking into their endless altercations sheds no real light on any of this. Sure, we get an entertaining earful of their especially grotesque specialities: brain-deep arrows, staff-beaten burglary victims, and dead bodies found at dawn, slumped against town walls with mutilated faces. But if we want to see past that, to learn about who clerks really were and why these murders happened, we have to come face to face with a young man named Roger.

We find ourselves in Oxford on Horsemonger Street on the day before the feast of St Catherine the Virgin, in the twenty-ninth year of King Edward I. You got that, right? This is how dates were written through the Middle Ages: the day is not given as a numerical date within the month, but referenced in its relation to the closest or most important holy day on the ecclesiastical calendar. So instead of a day being Tuesday 6 April, it's the Tuesday before Easter. Years did not make use of Anno Domini or Common Era dating, but were given in context of the reign of the current king[*] – this was known as the 'regnal year'. So instead of the date of AD 1300, it is the twenty-ninth year of King Edward I. But, to make things even *more* confusing, regnal years did not start at the same time as ecclesiastical ones did; the regnal year began on the anniversary of the king's ascension, meaning the start of the twenty-ninth regnal year of King Edward I was 20 November, while the start of 1300 Anno Domini was 25 March, or Lady Day.[†] Yeah. It's a big headache.

---

[*] 'Anno Domini' dating was not used much in the Middle Ages (at least not in this context) but AD is not unlike the sentiment behind the regnal year, as Jesus Christ is, according to the Bible, the King of Kings.

[†] This all gets even more complicated when leaving England, as different countries all had different dating practices.

Put simply in modern terms, our medieval scene takes place on 27 November in the year AD 1300.* It is evening, sometime before vespers, and the sun hovers low over the horizon. It would take another few decades for mechanical clocks to be widely in use, which means the hourly notation used in Roger's inquest, as well as the clocks chiming in the bell towers of Oxford, were using the solar hours. This system of time reckoning divided the hours of daylight into twelve equal hours, no matter how long the sun shone. Nighttime was likewise divided into twelve equal hours. This meant that daytime summer hours, with more time between sunrise and sunset, were much longer than winter hours, and the hours of the night in winter much longer than the hours of the night in summer.

Given that the term 'o'clock' didn't arise until the use of mechanical clocks – since it means *of the clock* – hours of the day were given different names. The first hour of the day was called 'prime' and began at sunrise. The third hour, roughly 9 a.m., was called 'terce'. The sixth hour of 'sext' followed at noon, with the ninth hour of 'nones' at 9 p.m. The whole day was wrapped up by 'vespers' at the twelfth hour, which took place at sunset. For Roger here on 27 November in Oxford, England, the bell for vespers would have rung at 4 p.m.

---

* I do not know if these dates converted by the original translators and editors of these inquests are given using the Julian or Gregorian calendar, but I am assuming it is the latter. If it is, for some reason, the Julian, this means my calculations for the solar hours are off by just a few minutes.

And so we have our scene. It's a chilly one, late afternoon by modern clocks, the sun beginning to set on the horizon. Horsemonger Street, now Broad Street, is crowded about by tall timber buildings casting their long shadows, the smell and sounds of horses and people filling in every corner between them. Smoke from countless fires drifts lazily through the air. Imagine, if you will, being just a pace behind Roger on this street as he makes his way to the Old Hall, or Baylolhall, as some may call it. We weave between the puddles, the people and piles of horse dung left by the stock that is bought, sold and traded here. The men we pass are in long woollen tunics and hose, and women dot the shadows with the clean white of their wimples and veils bobbing with their gaits like ghosts. Their clothes are all sorts of colours: blues from woad, reds from madder, yellows and greens from onion skin, marigold and weld. One or two men pass us with the distinct pattering of wooden pattens affixed to their soft leather shoes, protecting them from all the muck this time of year.

Unlike the clerks you may be used to, Roger is not on his way to pick a fight, nor is he brandishing some magnificent pole arm, looking to finally settle things here and now. He is simply on his way 'to have games with some scholars of his own district'. Yes, that's right – Roger's on his way to game night. We can assume all the medieval hits are there, including draughts,[*] chess, frequently-banned-because-they-got-too-

---

[*] Checkers, in some parts of the world.

violent dice games, and perhaps even 'le wraesteling', if we're to believe the evidence of other inquests.*

Roger makes it to game night at Baylolhall and the evening passes pleasantly for a while, without remark. There is likely drinking, for there is always likely to be drinking after dark in medieval England. And then Roger, in his innocence, makes his way up to the second storey of the hall. While lingering outside of a room in the gallery, he leans against the railing, which breaks, and he falls.

The fall does not kill him. His friends gather him up and rush him to his lodgings, but despite their care, it does not look good for poor Roger. He lies in bed for six days, having contracted a fever 'because of the anguish of the fall', and then dies, having had all his church rites. He was sixteen years old.

I know, you might be thinking – that's it? A guy fell down on game night and this is supposed to answer *all* our questions about clerks?

Well, you just have to know what and where the clues are.

This is the *only* report used for the bot that states the age of a clerk, which makes it not only remarkable, but thoroughly illuminating. If we piece his age together with the city he died in – Oxford – and the comment that he was going to hang out with 'fellow scholars', the identity of these clerks becomes immediately clear: they are undergrads at Oxford University.

---

* We know wrestling was a hit because, of course, it was involved in someone's death.

While it may be tempting to define the clerks in these inquests as clerics and then call it a day, the word 'clerk', or *clericus* in the Latin, does not seem to be used for the ecclesiastical sort in these reports, and to declare that slews of holy men were running around killing each other for no good reason paints an incredibly strange and inaccurate picture of medieval Oxford.

Most, if not all, of the clerks that make an appearance on the bot are the scholarly type of clerk, like Roger. 'Clerk' was a term widely used for anyone whose job included a lot of writing and record-keeping. Thusly there were scholarly clerks, like those in Oxford, as well as clerks of the court, clerks of coroners, even clerks who kept track of spices in royal kitchens. Most of the clerks mentioned in the bot were young students at Oxford, aged anywhere from fourteen to twenty-something,* likely a long way away from home, who had full access to not only alcohol, but weapons. Very sharp weapons. They roamed Catte Street† and Horsemonger Street, staffs and buckles and poleaxes in hand, looking to disturb the peace – and doing a fine job of it. They brood with what can really only be called the hubris and hot-headedness of youth. It's all bad plans, raging hormones, alcohol, daggers and prejudice.

Which takes us to our next point: Horsemonger Street.

---

* Possibly even older, if you were a law student.

† This street was likely spelled 'Kattestreete' in 1300. I do not have the original Latin for the inquest that mentions this street by name, however, so I cannot verify the spelling. The English translation of the inquest simply calls it 'Cat Street.'

Baylolhall Hall. 'Scholars of his own district'. Oxford accepted students from all over England, as well as from Wales, Ireland, Scotland and the Continent. Mentions of the clerks doing the murdering, or who have been murdered, often include their nationality, or which parish they belonged to. Robert de la Marche dies in 1300, murdered by an Irish clerk. The same fate is due Adam de Sarum in 1303 over a game of football. Gervase, a Welsh clerk, is murdered in 1300 in Takley's Inn* by clerks who are definitely *not* Welsh. It's been estimated that about 94 per cent of students at Oxford at this time were English,[1] leaving the remaining 6 per cent to either be targeted for their foreignness, or face overwhelming odds if they wanted to start some shit.

If clerks needed any additional help breeding contempt for their fellow students, Oxford followed the French model of universities and divided students into *nationes* depending on where they were from. In Oxford's early years there may have been four *nationes*, but they were ultimately condensed to just two: the *austriales* from the north, and the *borealis* from the south, with the river Trent acting as the defining line between the two.

As one may suspect, these *nationes* clashed, giving birth to spitting, hissing rivalries. Not even an attempt to ban them in 1274 stopped them from forming, or those involved from killing

---

* Takley's Inn (alternatively spelled Tackley's Inn) was situated at what is now 106 High Street in Oxford, where it somewhat remains as a Grade II* listed building, due to it being 'one of the very few examples of a medieval academic hall still surviving'.

each other. We have a vivid account from 1388 of some of the *borealis* who sought to slaughter the Welsh students of the *australes*. They rioted, looted and murdered, roaming the streets of Oxford chanting 'War, war, war, slay, slay, slay the Welsh dogs'. They ended the scene by gathering up the remaining survivors of their wrath and urinating on them before peacing the hell out.[2]

This wasn't the only method of division between clerks, however, and we see this hinted at in the comment that Roger went to Baylolhall Hall to play games with 'scholars of his own district who abode there'. Besides belonging to a northern or southern gang of sorts, students were housed in privately owned halls depending on their area of study. Roger – whose focus of study we don't get to hear about – goes to a separate hall to hang out with students from his region who are studying something other than he is. It doesn't take much of a stretch of the imagination to conclude that these separations could, in fact, breed even more contempt If you're a low sort of fellow with a grudge against someone, you'll accept any perceived difference as fuel for your petty little fire. Especially if you're only sixteen.

Roger, through whatever grace, does not experience such violence. He dies from an accidental fall – a 'misadventure'. There are no teenaged tempers here, no quarrels, no drawn weapons. It is exceptional for its relative peacefulness, and for just how much insight it gives us into who these men really were.

2

A TRAIL OF BLOOD

The Murders of Adam de Osegodby

from *Records of Medieval Oxford*

dam de Osegodby appears in the *Records of Medieval Oxford* not just once, but four separate times, like a comet streaking through the summer sky over Oxford, a quick flash against June's stars, sowing nothing but mayhem in its light. He is one of the few people to appear multiple times in a single coroners' roll as a central part of the action, and just as quickly as he appears from nowhere, so does he disappear into nothingness.

The first mention of Adam appears behind a robbery of a blue and burnet robe and three shillings of silver.[*] It is not Adam who has committed the crime, but a man by the auspicious-sounding name of John Murthur. In late February[†] of 1324, John

---

[*] As I am not a historian of economics, I can't begin to estimate inflation for this price. 'Burnet', I can say with confidence, however, is a shade of red.

[†] But possibly early March, as I'm unsure if the modern dates given have been adjusted to the Gregorian calendar or are still using the Julian. The date of the robbery in the inquest is given as 'the Friday after Ash Wednesday'.

Murthur, clerk, robs John le Bonde of Bernyton, a squire, on the high road between Wycombe and Beaconsfield. They are probably peers, John le Bonde as a squire being somewhere between fifteen and twenty-one, and John Murther likely the same, given the general age of the clerks swarming around Oxford. Why exactly one John robs the other is unknown to us, the coroner of this inquest perhaps not bothering to probe as to why, or the clerk omitting unnecessary detail, satisfied to note that the crime did happen, and by Murthur's very own admission.

On 2 June, three entire months later, it seems that the law has caught up with John Murthur's theft, and we find him doing what any clever lad would to buy himself some time before he gets caught: he seeks sanctuary in a church. Sanctuary was a right given to felons, usually who had committed capital offences, to be given the protection of the church instead of likely being sentenced to death. If it was determined by the government that they deserved the church's protection for their crimes, they had the option to forego capital punishment and instead become an exile.[1]

This specific kind of exile for capital offences was known as 'abjuration of the realm', and it meant that, because John had stolen a robe and three silver shillings and did not want to die for it, he would be forced to leave England,* barefoot and

---

* Supposedly, felons were given the 'choice' of which port they wanted to disembark from. However, it is clear from reports that it was usually up to the coroner in question, and the port of choice was almost always Bristol.

bareheaded, all his earthly goods being given over to the crown and the church, and never return. If he ever did come back to England during the reign of the current king, he would be put to death.[2]

These abjuration cases are the only non-death entries to appear in coroners' rolls. Their inclusion gives us a stark idea of the perception of such a punishment at the time. Abjuration was the mark and acknowledgement of a mortal sin – it may as well have been death.

This was the intended fate for John Murthur, but it is not what happened.

After spending one single night of sanctuary in St Mildred's, John breaks from the church by 'the council and aid of Adam de Osegodby, clerk, and others whose names are unknown'. Now, aiding someone in breaking sanctuary was indeed a criminal offence, and while some might think it smart to lay low after such a scene, Adam's crimes, instead, escalate.

We find Adam next mixed up in murder. It is 8 June, only about a week since he helped John Murthur out of St Mildred's, and he, along with his buddy Richard Wakelyn, are roaming the streets sometime between curfew and midnight, armed and ready. There is no mention of whether the assault on Richard Overhe, a constable of the peace, is premeditated or not, but they beat him soundly in the street with 'swords, bucklers and other arms'. The fatal blow is a wound beneath the ear. Richard does not die immediately from this wound, but lingers for twenty-four miserable days until 2 July, when he dies in his home.[*]

At this point the inquests become unclear in their dating, making the exact sequence of events hard to pin down. What is certain is that around midnight on either 7 or 8 June Adam, with eight other clerks in tow,[†] meets John de Staunford le Shereman somewhere on his prowl, and smites him 'in the breast with a piece of iron fixed in the end of a staff'.[‡] It is a sufficient blow; John dies a month later, on 2 July, the same night as Richard Overhe.

With so much violence, murder and crime staining his hands, it seems unlikely that Adam could escape this violence in his own end. And so we find one last entry mentioning the man.

On Friday 8 June 1324, Adam de Osegodby is found dead in the high street near the north gate of Oxford, his murder occurring likely just a few hours after the assault on Richard Overhe. He is stabbed with a dagger in the stomach, just below the navel, by Ernald Flyngaunt, a man guarding a felon who had fled to a church seeking sanctuary – likely a felon

---

[*] A note in the original translation of these rolls dating from 1912 states that Richard Overhe's home is 'now the Three Cups on Queen Street'. Today, the Three Cups is a Nationwide Building Society.

[†] They are: Richard Wlkeylyn, Thomas Manciple del Castellhall, Robert de St Mor, Benedictus de Carleolo, Robert de Heselbech, William de Kyllum, William de Aldwykes and Adam de Howton.

[‡] This would be some form of poleaxe, but it is curious that it is not called that in the report. Was the clerk feeling cheeky?

that Adam had come to break out. But there is no comment to motive, and no description of the fight between them in the inquest. We are given only the most basic of information: he is stabbed in the stomach, and found dead in the street.[*] Ernald flees under the cover of night. And so Adam disappears from these rolls as he disappeared from life, one of the most unscholarly clerks of Oxford.

---

[*] It is likely that Adam was killed outside the church of St Michael at the North Gate, putting his death on what is now Cornmarket or Ship Street, as it seems that versions of these streets did exist in the fourteenth century.

3

JOHN WICK GOES MEDIEVAL

The Death of William Baman

from *Calendar of Coroners Rolls of the City of London*

o set the stage for the death of William Baman, we must take a detour first to the tale of Auberie of Moundydier and his noble greyhound.

Auberie* was a squire of the king's house of France, and upon a day that he was going from the court to his own house, and as he passed by the woods of Bondis, the which is nigh Paris, and led with him a well good and a fair greyhound that he had brought up. A man that hated him for great envy without any other reason, who was called Makarie, ran upon him within the wood and slew him without warning, for Auberie was not aware of him. And when the greyhound sought his master and found him he

---

* *The Master of Game* spells this as 'Aubery' and 'Auberie'. I have taken the liberty of standarising it to 'Auberie' for consistency.

covered him with earth and with leaves with his claws and his muzzle in the best way that he could. And when he had been there three days and could no longer abide for hunger, he turned again to the king's court.

There he found Makarie, who was a great gentleman, who had slain his master, and as soon as the greyhound perceived Makarie, he ran upon him, and would have maimed him, unless men had hindered him. The King of France, who was wise and a man of perception, asked what it was, and men told him the truth. The greyhound took from the boards what he could, and brought to his master and put meat in his mouth, and the same wise the greyhound did three days or four. And then the King made men follow the greyhound, for to see where he bare the meat that he took in the court. And then they found Auberie dead and buried.

And then the King, as I have said, made come many of the men of his court, and made them stroke the greyhound's side, and cherish him and made his men lead him by the collar towards the house, but he never stirred. And then the King commanded Makarie to take a small piece of flesh and give it to the greyhound. And as soon as the greyhound saw Makarie, he left the flesh, and would have run upon him. And when the King saw that, he had great suspicions about Makarie, and said [to] him that he must needs fight against the greyhound. And Makarie began to laugh, but anon the King made him do the deed, and one of the kinsmen of Auberie saw the great marvel of the greyhound and said that he would swear upon the sacrament as is the custom in such a case for the greyhound, and Makarie swore on the other side, and then they were led into our Lady's Isle at Paris and there fought the greyhound and Makarie. For which Makarie had a great two-handed staff, and they fought so that Makarie was discomfited, and then the King commanded that the greyhound the which had Makarie under him should be taken up, and then the King made enquiry of the truth of Makarie, the which acknowledged he had slain Auberie in treason, and therefore he was hanged and drawn.[1]

The tale is one of stupendous loyalty and cunning – and, of course, probably not true. It is recounted in the fourteenth-century *The Master of Game*, the oldest hunting book in the English language,[*] which is profuse with praise for dogs.

---

[*] *The Master of Game* can't be considered a wholly original work, however, as much of it was translated from the early fifteenth-century French book *Livre de Chasse* by Count Gaston de Foix (also known as Gaston Fébus or Gaston Phoebus).

They are noble, loyal, hardy, diligent, strong and wise, kind and obedient, and as prized as much as a lady's lapdog as they are a hunting beast. A thirteenth-century bestiary agrees heartily with *The Master of Game* that dogs can, and do, involve themselves in the judiciary system, stating that 'dogs have often provided persuasive evidence which has led to the conviction of [a] criminal, and their silent testimony can usually be believed.'[2]

It is with this love and reverence for the humble hound that we approach the house of Philip de Spine on 7 July 1301. It is dark – after curfew, as the report says – and Philip is there with his neighbour, William Baman de Chaurede, his steward, Touse le Lumbard, and his beloved hounds. We can imagine them gathered around the hearth, burning lowly in the summer night, the dogs lazily stretched out around it as their master entertains (or perhaps just *puts up with*) William Baman.

This scene is interrupted when one of Philip's dogs starts a fight with another. It may have been just a snarl, or a full-on scrap – the report doesn't tell us. All we know is that William, either attempting to quell or chastise them, oversteps and 'savagely' strikes one of the dogs.

In doing so, he seals his own fate.

Philip, 'moved to anger', begins to 'rate the said William'. At this cue, Philip's steward steps in with a balstaf* and beats the

---

* A 'balstaff' goes by many names in the Middle Ages (balghstaff, balkstaff) and seems to be little more than a wooden staff.

man. He strikes his arms and shoulders over and over, beating him hard enough that Philip and Touse have to flee the next day when they get word that the man is near death. William lingers for three days, lasting until Monday, 'when he died of the beating at dawn'.

The corpse, when examined, has a swollen and inflamed right arm, and the body is blue with bruises between the shoulders.

Philip and Touse are never seen again, and their chattels given up.

It is a death such as this that makes us wonder that perhaps what we admire in dogs is what we aspire to ourselves. Loyalty, indeed.

4

FOUL TREDEKEILES

The Death of Walter de Elmeleye

from *Select Cases from the Coroners' Rolls A.D. 1265–1413*

e find ourselves now in London on a warm summer's night in 1301. It is after vespers,[*] and Alice le Quernbeter is drunk. She walks down Selverstrete to the corner of Wodestrete,[†] where she encounters a handful of construction workers preparing the ground for a new home. 'Being drunk', as the report explains, she insults and abuses them, calling them at one point 'tredekeiles', an insult that enrages one of the men so much that he comes over, grabs her hand, retorts that she can 'work and tread the ground with them' if she wants, and then 'maliciously' shoves her onto the ground.

Both pissed and pissed off, Alice goes straight home.

---

[*] During the summer season of plentiful daylight, vespers would have been around 7 p.m.

[†] 'Silver Street' and 'Wood Street', respectively. Wood Street is still called this today.

And comes back with her landlady,[*] Elene Hellbole. She is entirely on Alice's side, and starts yelling at the workmen herself, 'calling them Ribalds and other opprobrious names'. One of the men 'whose name they know not' starts yelling at Elene. She calls him a thief, he calls her a whore. It enrages Elene enough to threaten that before night comes, the matter shall be settled.

So she sends for Walter the Chaplain, as well as a tenant of hers named Roger le Skirmisour, and 'another person unknown' to avenge her on this 'said stranger' who called her a whore. Despite not knowing who he is, as the report claims, they know he is now at Agnes de Notingham's tavern, and they hightail it there, stopping for a moment to buy a 'fagot for a farthing, from which each man furnished himself with a stick'.

Armed with their sticks, they arrive at the tavern and meet John de Melkesham, who seems to be the offender they're looking for. Walter the Chaplain asks the man if he has abused Elene, and instead of answering, John strikes Walter on his head and arm. John draws a dagger, and Walter, seeing it, reaches to grab his knife, but is too slow. John stabs Walter 'under the shoulder, inflicting a wound an inch and a half broad and reaching to the heart'. Walter then 'immediately dies'.

---

[*] The inquest uses the word 'mistress', which I have substituted (though it is not a perfect match).

After killing a man, John flees to the church of St Olave,[*] seeking sanctuary for his crime, only to end up escaping later that night.

So we go from drunkenly flinging insults to murdering a chaplain. A typical medieval summer night? Well – probably not. That this scene escalates towards murder seems to suggest strange things about our medieval forebears – that they were more prone to violence than we are now, or that they lived with a perpetual bloodlust attached to a very short fuse. Or perhaps it proves that they were too overly sensitive to insults and needed to just toughen up a bit. You know, sticks and stones and all that.

The reality, I believe, is something quite different, but it takes time to unravel.

One of our huge disconnects from the medieval world, the gap in which a thousand misinterpretations can bloom, is the difference in literacy rates and just how that impacts a society. Literacy rates in fourteenth-century England are difficult to define – there is certainly no census data for such a thing, and just which languages in use counted for literacy at that time is hard to pin down[†] – but it is plain to see that there was no

---

[*] This church still exists on Hart Street in the City of London. It was one of the few medieval churches to survive the Great Fire of 1666. It is about a mile away (by modern roads) from the approximate location of Alice's altercation with the workmen on Wood Street.

[†] At this time, the nobility were still speaking Anglo-Norman, a version of French brought over from the Conquest. It was not until the reign of Edward III that English was embraced by the nobility (and even then, some were slow to adopt it). Latin, of course, was also used by some members of society, but not as a first language.

expectation of those of the lower classes, which made up most of the population, to learn how to read and write. They were, however, expected to enter into legally binding contracts, be they marriage or service to a lord, as well as having civic duties to appear in courts. The legal system was prepared to deal with this illiteracy, and it did so with the swearing of oaths.

It is this oath-swearing that not only gives us the term *swearing* to mean saying foul or rude words, but added a gravity to things you said.* You stood by your promises, your oaths, your accusations. If you called someone a thief, it wasn't just an insult, but could be taken as an accusation of a crime punishable by death, and a statement that perhaps needed to be examined in a civil court of law.†

So when the worker called Alice a whore, it was serious. And when Alice called the construction worker a tredekeil it was also serious, because she accused him of being… well, *something* awful.

The exact meaning of the word 'tredekeil' is somewhat of a head-scratcher, partially because the only recorded use of this exact word is from this very inquest. A Middle English dictionary I consulted simply defines it as a 'term of abuse',

---

* While modern swearing focuses on words that have been deemed rude or coarse, medieval swearing revolved around the vain taking of an oath in sight of God without meaning it, which corrupted the body of Christ in heaven. 'Shit' was not a bad word in 1301, but swearing the oath that 'by God's bones' you'd do something you had no intention of doing had serious consequences on the bones of God (or Jesus), which was important because he was the one who controlled where you would be spending your eternal life. Best to mean what you say, then.

† This is not to suggest that no one had a sense of humour, or that every statement was taken as bold truth. The reality exists somewhere in the middle.

citing this inquest for support of that definition, but doesn't dive into *why* it's an insult. In further research, I found it being insufficiently defined both as 'pavement stompers' and 'lousy slobs', the former a more literal interpretation, the latter possibly more euphemistic, but without either definition being sourced or explained. This didn't satisfy me – I wanted to get at not just what it actually meant, but why it was so upsetting. So I spent months ruminating on it, digging around in more dictionaries and books, and asking my friends who keep birds weird questions to get to the heart of it.

One of our most important clues is that the word appears in the inquest in quotation marks. The original coroners' reports were written in medieval Latin, this specific roll being translated into Modern English in the late nineteenth century, and these quotation marks imply that the word was in English in the original report. This hints that the word only functions in English, literally and/or euphemistically, and that it is untranslatable into Latin; subsequent insults in the report such as *thief* and *whore* have easy Latin equivalents, so they are translated, and do not appear in quotes.

If 'tredekeils' needs to remain in English, it is possibly idiomatic, or works with dual meanings that only make sense in English. The word contains the Middle English 'trēden', which means to tread or stomp – hence the literal translation of it as 'pavement stompers'. And we see support of this more literal meaning in the inquest, with the workman retorting to

Alice that she 'should work and tread the ground with them' before 'maliciously bumping' her to the ground. But such a word is hardly offensive. Imagine being Alice in this scene: you're drunk, the work day's over, and you're having yourself a nice stroll down the street, and you see some men working on a building site that you don't like the look of. You decide to yell out at them – 'Hey pavement stompers! I see you! You... lousy pavement stompers, you!'

Unless there is some uproarious stigma I don't know about surrounding workmen who laid foundations in the Middle Ages, it doesn't really work as an insult by any more literal definition. Alice's calling out is a nuisance, perhaps, but we can imagine the workmen shrugging and going back to their work, trying to ignore the drunk woman yelling inane things at them. It is hard to imagine one of them striding over, chatting back and knocking her to the ground for it.

The word 'trēden', however, like the modern word 'tread', has a secondary, slightly more obscure meaning, applied to the mating of birds. A male bird mating with a female is called 'treading', even today. This more salacious meaning was in use in application to humans in the late Middle Ages as well. Chaucer uses it in 'The Monk's Tale' to call someone a 'chicken fucker,'* and it appears idiomatically in the phrase 'woman who has never trod her shoe amiss' – meaning she has never been unchaste.

---

* A 'tredefowl', which prudes define as 'chicken copulater'. Other sources cite it as being a 'jocular' term for a 'sexually vigorous' man.

So a 'tredekeil' is some sort of horny fucker. This is the insult that Alice comes over and flings to the workers: they're a handful of *horny guys*. Within a braid of other unknown insults, this can be seen as quite horrendous. It undermines their manhood, and thereby their station above women. For nothing is more horrifying in a fragile, patriarchal society than the suggestion that one is not of the 'rightfully dominant' gender.

It is no secret that the Middle Ages was a rampantly misogynistic era. Reigning medical texts, philosophical thinkers and church fathers alike viewed women as the lesser form of man.* Thomas Aquinas called women 'defective and misbegotten'; their physical state, Aristotle said, should be seen as a 'deformity', and thusly, they were 'properly' subject to men because they were physically and morally vulnerable, and lacking in judgement.[1] Some of this lack of judgement was their wantonness, and as the German scholar Albertus Magnus, writing in the late thirteenth or early fourteenth century, pointed out, this wantonness grew from a desire to join with man, a perfect being, since the imperfect always desires to be perfected. This longing for sex seemed to be a pungent, ever-present desire, fed by unspent menses within the womb, and it led women to repeatedly tempt men into carnal deeds; in doing so they were all Eve again, tempting Adam to eat the forbidden fruit.

---

* It is more correctly said that this was the opinion of anyone assigned female at birth, since medieval society had not yet separated the body from gender.

If this was not harsh enough, the thirteenth-century canonist Cardinal Hostiensis admitted that a husband must give in to these desires so that the 'weak, readily stimulated creatures'[2] would not be driven astray by their rampant sex drive into committing adultery, a sin that some women were *too stupid to realise was a sin at all*. Yikes.

So, a tredekiel was no small deal. While literally retaining a 'tread' or 'stomp' prefix, it euphemistically delivers the sentence of being a horny fucker. Which, if you're a thin-skinned man highly invested in maintaining the patriarchal status-quo in the fourteenth century, is just horrendous. It's like guys who think 'pussy' is an insult!

We are, of course, missing the second half of the word, as I could not find any satisfactory definition for 'kiel', or any similar-sounding word that could result in such a spelling in English. The offence of being called horny has to be considered alongside some unknown variables. For example, what were the other insults given by Alice? Was this the first time Alice had insulted the workers, or was this a common occurrence? Was this an altercation attached to a very long fuse? Was the word 'tredekiel' really *that* inflammatory? Or was it only mentioned to explain the retort of the workman in saying that she could come tread the ground with them if she wished? Sadly, we'll never know the whole story. The insult in the inquest remains an example of some pretty clever wordplay, but did it really need to end with the murder of an innocent chaplain? Probably not.

5

THE PENETRATED FUNDAMENT

The Death of Henry Constentin

from Select Cases from the Coroners' Rolls A.D. 1265–1413

ow this death is just bad luck. On 11 August 1267, Henry Constentin is driving a horse-drawn cart of wheat through the field of Tweedscroft near what is now Eaton Socon in Cambridgeshire. Agnes Ansell, a woman whose relationship to Henry is in no way explained in the report, is with him when his feet slip and he falls upon 'a certain pole' of his cart 'so that it penetrate[s] into his fundament'. He dies of the wound four days later around the hour of prime.*

Like many men before him and many men after him, Henry falls to his death carting through a field. But unlike a lot of them, the wreck causes him to get impaled up the ass so

---

* The original translation of these inquests gives a time of 6 a.m.; however, the actual hour of prime for 11 August 1267 would've started around 4:32 a.m.

bad he dies from it. And I really do think it was right up the ass. The original Latin in the inquest states that this certain pole '*intravit ad fundamentum*', which literally means 'enters into his bottom', the word 'fundament' able to mean either buttocks or anus. Here it could very well mean anus, given the preposition 'into' and the severity of the wound, which likely caused Henry's death by loss of blood through internal bleeding. Had he simply been hit by a pole in his butt muscle, he probably wouldn't have died.

But impalement aside, just how in the world did this accident happen in the first place? Was carting through fields really that dangerous, or was Henry just fatally bad at his job?

You might be surprised to hear that carting through fields was the number one cause of accidental death when it comes to agricultural work in the late Middle Ages.[1] It was not only slightly more fatal than other kinds of agricultural work, but two and a half times more dangerous than the runner-up for agricultural related deaths (which is working with animals, if you're curious).

Turns out, carting through a field with a towering pile of wheat was no joke. Standard transportation alone in the Middle Ages was risky, accounting for 43 per cent of men's fatal accidents for the era.[2] Roads were uneven and badly maintained, with precarious potholes, puddles, and dangerous drainage ditches on either side, which claimed plenty of lives on their own. Carts and wagons flipped, got stuck, overturned and broke on these roads, and roads were the land *meant* for travel. Pulling a cart of hay through a field was an entirely different story. Cartloads had to be loaded with even weight distribution, and they were often loaded to towering heights, necessitating the use of a ladder. Careless loading and tying down of these carts could, and sometimes did, result in broken necks.

An illustration from the Luttrell Psalter, made in 1325–40, about sixty years after Henry's death, gives us a good idea of what Henry driving his cart would've looked like. In it, three harnessed horses pull a large blue cart carrying a heaping load of wheat which towers as tall as the driver, who stands with one foot placed precariously on each cart shaft that connects to the horses' harnesses. The load itself is secured to the cart with four ropes, and three people assist the cart along: one at the wheel close to us, ensuring it rotates properly, with two behind the cart helping the sheaves stay put for their journey. It paints a clear picture of just how insecure these cartloads could be, and how much of a concern it was that they did not tip.

It is in this scene we can assume Henry was both driving the horse and attempting to maintain his balance as the wheels went over the ground, the weight of the cart tipping and swaying behind him. He had to keep his eye on the horse – we have mention of a single horse in Henry's report, not a team of three as in the Luttrell illustration – and on Agnes, assisting him through the field, as well as keeping an eye out for other workers and carts in the field. With all the pieces in place, it's easy to see why and how Henry slipped, and why it was such a common occurrence.

The pole, however, we can only guess at. The report calls it a 'certain pole', failing to explain what kind of pole that is, or where it was situated so that it ended up in his ass. It seems reasonable to guess that the pole could have been a pitchfork stuck into the sheaves behind him, and he slipped and fell backwards upon it. Or something could have gone wrong with the harness on the horse, or the shafts connecting to it. The harness breaks, a shaft snaps, and the cart detaches from the horse. Henry loses his footing and falls onto the ground face-first, and the cart still rolls, tipped downwards, and manages to really ram the pole in there.

However it happened, Henry Constentin's life came to a most gruesome end.

Of course, with as sparse information is in this report, we can conjecture quite easily, filling in the gaps of the story with marvellously juicy ideas. I leave you with the tantalising fact that most village homicides happened in fields during the Autumn harvest,[3] and we can all wonder... just who was Agnes, and what was she really up to out there with Henry?

6

DEATH BY PISS

The Death of Philip de Asshendone
from *Calendar of Coroners Rolls of the City of London*

 f you're ever in London on Foster Lane near the church of St Vedast, you may want to pay respects to Philip de Asshendone, a man who was beaten to death on 8 December 1321 for attempting to help a stranger.

The street was called St Vedast Row back then, and during the hour of vespers – around 4 p.m. or so in winter – a man named William, son of Henry atte Row, was there, pissing into a urinal. But he wasn't just pissing – 'he cast [his] urine into the shoe of an unknown young man', the report says, 'and because the latter complained, the said William struck him with his fist'.

So, a pretty straightforward interaction here. William pisses into another man's shoe, who understandably hates that his shoe is being pissed in, especially given that his foot is currently in that shoe. But William hates that this guy hates it, so he punches him. This causes the pissed-on man to drop the 'pollex'* he was holding in his hand to the ground. Philip de Asshendone is our nearby Good Samaritan in this scene, and steps in to 'upbraid' William for pissing on and then punching another man. But William is having none of it. He wants to piss in other men's shoes and he won't hear any grief about it. So he does what any completely sane piss-lover would do: 'he straightway pick[s] up the staff and feloniously [strikes] the said [Philip]† over the forehead, inflicting a mortal wound an inch long and penetrating to the brain.' Philip falls to the ground, where he is picked up by 'unknown men' and taken to the hospital of St Mary without Bishopsgate.‡ There he has his ecclesiastical rites and then lingers 'until Saturday after the Feast of Circumcision, when he died at the third hour of the said wound and of no other felony'. This puts his death at 1 January 1322, an entire twenty-four days after the beating. What happened to the unknown man whose shoe got pissed in is unknown. As for William, he gets sent to Newgate Prison. And we can only hope that the unknown man's shoe was the last he ever pissed in.

* Probably a poleaxe, which is just what it sounds like: a long pole with an axe head on the end of it.
† The report erroneously states that William strikes William with the staff, when it is clearly Philip that has been hit by William.
‡ Founded in 1197 and originally known as Blessed Virgin Mary without Bishopsgate. Through the years it's also been called New Hospital of St Mary without Bishopsgate, St Mary without Bishopsgate and St Mary Spital – 'spital' here being old slang for 'hospital'.

THE SOW WAS ARRESTED

The Death of Agnes Perone

from *Records of Medieval Oxford*

n Genesis, the Christian God creates man and gives him dominion over the earth and all the animals upon it, establishing a firm hierarchy of God, man and beast. In Exodus, he details the punishment for animals that upset that hierarchy by taking the life of a human; they are to be publicly stoned to death, and their flesh thrown away, not to be eaten.[1] And so, in accordance with Biblical law, documented cases of animals being put to trial for their crimes against mankind appear as early as the ninth century in Europe. Thomas Aquinas, writing in the thirteenth century, was the first to question the actual guilt of these animals, and came to the conclusion that while some beasts were God's creatures, the guilty ones surely belonged to the devil,[2] and that it was no blasphemy against God to condemn them to a death that would send them to their master. So justified, the trend of putting animals on trial thus continued up until the nineteenth century in England and all across Europe, and it's easy to see why when we look at the death of Agnes Perone.

It is 7 May 1392, and little Agnes, half a year old, is asleep in her cradle near the fire. The home she is in is small and dark, wattle and daub and thatch-roofed; a simple structure with a short lifespan. Sunshine pours in through the open door and the unglazed window, twirling in the smoke that lazily makes its way up and out, free from any flue. Outside, birds chatter and call, men and women work, children play amongst kale gardens and squawking hens, and the family sow bathes herself in the cool mud.

Today, Satan makes use of that sow.

She wanders in through the open door of the Perones' house and finds little Agnes alone in her cradle. She then eats Agnes' head 'even to the nose', killing her. In reaction to Agnes' death, an inquest is held that very afternoon, and instead of giving the sow a deodand price to be paid to the crown, the sow is arrested.

Agnes' death is monumental in meaning. It is profoundly disturbing in its own right, conjuring up horrible imagery. Yet the report of her death is terribly brief, giving us only a few bare facts to reconstruct the scene. The arrest of the sow at the end, where we usually expect to find a deodand price, acts as a bizarre punchline to the non-joke, almost as if it is an attempt to turn the whole thing into a comedy. But there is no joke here. Agnes' death instead highlights the tragedy of the working poor, and gives us proof that the bizarrely righteous tradition of putting animals on trial was, in fact, alive in England in the fourteenth century.

In the Norman city of Falaise six years previous, a sow stood trial for maiming a five-year-old boy to death. In 1266, a pig from Fontenay-aux-Roses in France was executed for its crimes, and in 1463 in Amiens, two pigs were buried alive for having 'torn and eaten with their teeth a little child'.[3] Most of the animals that saw the executioner's axe were pigs, and most of them in France. But all across Europe and England, pigs outweighed all other offenders, the numbers of murderous swine double the total of all other offending animals on record from the thirteenth to the sixteenth centuries. I cannot explain it except to say that they had (or perhaps still have?) a worrying preference for the taste of babies and children. And while the scene of Agnes' death was a common one, such attacks were not always fatal. In the episcopal records of Lincoln exists a copy of a certificate issued at the request of a woman who wanted the world to know that she had lost one of her ears not as punishment for any misdeed on her part, but because a sow had bitten it off when she was a baby.[4]

Apart from pigs, vermin also wreaked havoc, destroying crops with 'felonious intent', as a medieval coroner's clerk might phrase it. This, too, was a horrible, unforgivable crime that demanded justice – but instead of executing the offending vermin via a trial in a civil court, they were instead excommunicated by the church. It was impossible to effectively gather and contain pests such as swarming locusts in order for them to stand trial in a civil court. Indeed, if it had been so easy to contain and control these pests, there wouldn't have been any crop destruction in the first place. So pests and vermin were regarded as acts of God, and man was as helpless against them as they were against a drought. Only God's justice could be applied to them, and excommunication was the harshest divine punishment that could be wrought.

You might be wondering – what did excommunicating locusts actually *do*? They certainly weren't eradicated by what amounted to little more than ritual cursing, so why even bother?

Simply put, the public executions of animals and excommunication of offending vermin served not only as a theological exercise, but as meaningful ritual for the suffering community. It allowed those who partook, be they grieving, starving or horrified by the maiming of an infant or small child, to reinforce their dominance over what was below them, to get back some modicum of control in a world where they were helpless against so much. For the medieval community, especially in light of a death like Agnes', it was important to right the world, and righting it demanded that man ruled over beasts and vermin with the same cruel and righteous justice that God ruled over man.

So the sow that killed Agnes is arrested, and the world is righted. But how did it manage to wander in and kill Agnes in the first place?

Agnes was killed in early May, the start of the busiest season for outside labour, demanding huge volumes of work from both parents. There wasn't much time to dedicate solely to baby-minding, and while socially frowned upon, infants and young children sometimes had to be left alone while parents worked.* Efforts to secure them from crawling about and getting into things they shouldn't while they were alone were made, such as swaddling and tying them into their cradles, but sometimes those methods were ineffective at keeping them from harm. Robert, son of Walter, one and a half years old, was left tied in his cradle when a fire started. Unable to get out and escape the flames, it killed him.[5]

Some parents brought swaddled infants and young children out to the fields with them, but this was not always practical. Their presence would have been a distracting one, and could have had a negative impact on their parents' productivity. Moreover, field work was not the only thing to be done, and many jobs could not offer a relatively secure or convenient place to put a swaddled infant. For some tasks, the only real option was leaving the baby at home and praying that everything would be alright.

* Or, in some cases, attended church. This does not seem to be the case with Agnes, however.

Baby-minding was similarly rare due to the demand for all who were able to work to work. Female children often became valuable aids for their mothers, picking up household chores as young as the age of six. Young boys, left free from labour a little longer due to their inability to perform as effectively as their fathers, could be reckless and careless. Those who were good candidates to watch a small child had other things to do – and so babies were often left in the care of siblings as young as three years old, or those unfit in other ways, such as the old blind woman who was set to watch Maude, daughter of William Bigge, while her mother visited a neighbour. Under her care, Maude wandered off and drowned in a ditch.[6]

So Agnes was left alone, swaddled in her cradle, sitting by the fire. Her inquest gives no account of where her parents were at the time, but it is easy to imagine her mother out fetching water, her father far away working in the fields. She either had no older siblings to mind her, or they, too, were working to help keep the household running. One important part of that household could have been the keeping of a pig; they were easy animals to maintain, unpicky with their food, satisfied with a little space of their own in the family croft, and infinitely useful. The inquest makes no mention of whose pig it was, the Perones' or a neighbour's. Whether or not Satan really used it, the sow was there, and the door was open. And so little Agnes died, and the sow was arrested. No documentation of the sow's trial follows this inquest, as it would be out of place in a coroners' roll, but we can rest assured that the pig, if it really did go to trial, was put to death for its crimes.

8

A PIT FULL OF SHIT

The Death of John Funke

from *Records of Medieval Oxford*

t is 10 July 1346, and for the death of John Funke, we find ourselves outside Oxford proper, on the grounds of the great Oseney[*] Abbey. The abbey is long gone now – only a ruined gate and a handful of crumbling walls near Bridge Street in Oxford still stand. But in the fourteenth century it stood tall and proud, flourishing as one of the wealthiest Oxfordshire monasteries, 'not only the envy of other religious houses, but of most beyond the sea.'[1]

It was here, on a moonlit summer's night at about midnight, that a man named John Funke arose from his sick bed and, 'for he was as it were mad', decided to start wandering about 'for want of guarding'. His good, if misguided, intentions

---

[*] Also spelled 'Osney'

led him into a pen* in the close† of the abbot of Oseney, where he fell into a cesspit and drowned.

John Funke's death mirrors many similar late-night ditch deaths of the late Middle Ages, but amongst the deep, watery ditches that many a drunken wanderer met their death in, latrines and cesspits rarely rear their head. Furthermore, the mention of a cesspit at Oseney Abbey seems out of character for the time and place – plumbing was entirely standard in monasteries by the fourteenth century, and the plumbing of Oseney would've followed the standard practice of waste removal by carrying it to a nearby source of running water, which the abbey, situated on the island of Oseney between a fork of the Thames, was surrounded by. Archaeological digs done in the 1970s and 1980s, as well as first-hand accounts of the buildings still standing post-Dissolution, confirm that the abbey was quite near the waterfront, with some buildings having to be rebuilt in the fourteenth century to move them further away from an eroding coastline.[2] So it does not seem implausible that these sources of running water could have been reached. And yet, there is a cesspit.

You might be wondering, then: perhaps John Funke fell into something else entirely. Perhaps there was an error made

---

* The inquest calls this a 'stode', which is a pen for holding livestock. It is likely it was either horses or sheep, though I can find no hard evidence for one over the other. The frequent presence of monasteries in the manufacturing of wool suggest it was likely sheep.

† A 'close' is simply private property, enclosed by a hedge or fence.

when the original medieval Latin was translated. Did they mean latrine, perhaps? Or midden? Or was this cesspit actually just one of many lethal ditches that littered the medieval world?

When it comes to this inquest, we actually have the original Latin placed in parenthesis after the word cesspit to clear up any confusion. The word is 'sterkulinio', a medieval bastardisation of the Latin word 'sterquilinium', which meant either 'dungheap/hill' or 'cesspit'. And while a dungheap (or midden) would have been entirely in place in a livestock pen, with or without intention to use it for manuring,* there's no possible way John could have *drowned* in one. There is also no evidence for, or sense in, creating a midden contained in a pit, since its contents would have needed to be shovelled and carted away to spread in furlongs. It can therefore be inferred that it contained something that was not needed, like human waste, which had no use in manuring.†

So, based on *sterkulinio* and the death-by-drowning, we undeniably have a cesspit on our hands. The simple answer may just have been that the abbot of Oseney was a big enough deal to want – and get – his own private shit house. The man was a Member of Parliament, after all. If he wanted his own latrine with a big ol' cesspit, he would get one.

---

* Manuring is the practice of using animal dung as fertiliser for crops. Walter of Henley, writing in the thirteenth century, suggests that manuring should be done 'before the drought of March'. As it was July at the time of John's death, even if there was a dungheap, it would not have been used for manuring.

† Stale urine, however, has long had use in laundering, as it turns into ammonia.

The rest of the scene is easy to put together. John Funke, sick as he was, would have been staying in the abbey's infirmary. Neither his madness nor his malady are specified in the inquest, but we can be sure that they were treated as one and the same, as madness in the late Middle Ages was seen as a symptom of a physical ailment. Conditions such as frenzy, melancholia and mania all had hardwired physical root causes. Yellow bile abscessing hotly in the brain caused frenzy. Mania was induced by an excessive diet. And vaporous black bile issuing forth from the stomach upwards to the brain could be responsible for a spell of melancholy.[*]

John's residence at the abbey furthermore informs us that while he may have been 'mad', he was not a lunatic, as many charitable foundations explicitly excluded such people.[3] Only a handful of foundations in England accepted lunatics – most notably St Mary Bethlehem in London,[†] which in 1403 housed six 'lunatics' as well as three sick persons. It seems that John Funke was physically ill, and perhaps suffering from a spell of madness (frenzy, as they would've called it) from a fever, or perhaps some form of physical trauma.

Thanks to anecdotal evidence of the remains of the abbey post-Dissolution, we have a vague idea of how the abbey may have been laid out, and providing that the layout of the abbey's

---

[*] This is by no means an extensive list. But it should be noted that most mental illnesses were *not* seen as having divine or demonic causes in the late Middle Ages.

[†] St Mary Bethlehem, founded in 1247, is not only still in operation as Bethlem Royal Hospital, but also gives us the term 'bedlam', based on its nickname.

many buildings didn't change *too* radically from the fourteenth to the sixteenth centuries,* the abbot's lodgings would have been in the southern part of the abbey grounds, just beneath the infirmary. It would have been an easy path for John to take, and one that did not require him to cross any of the waterways that surrounded the abbey.

So we can recreate the scene easily enough up to this point. Feverish and frenzied, John wakes up and decides to go out, perhaps to re-enact an old job as sentry, and wanders out into the night, where he ends up on the grounds of the abbot's residence. He then makes his way into a sheep pen and encounters a fateful latrine. It is likely he attempted to use it and then fell in, owing either to illness or madness. Either way, the man known as John Funke met his death, and it was in a pit full of shit.

---

* Oseney Abbey was founded in 1129, raised to the rank of abbey in 1154, and was rebuilt largely in the mid-thirteenth century during the abbacy of John Leech. We can assume, since there is no further mention of large-scale rebuilding, that the abbey retained a similar layout until the Dissolution.

9

DRUNK BEYOND MEASURE

The Death of Margery Golde

from Records of Medieval Oxford

Poor Margery. She probably never expected to find a small amount of fame 718 years after a night of being 'drunk beyond measure' and burning to death in her sleep, yet here we are. Her death is always a favourite whenever it comes up on the bot, garnering handfuls of replies and quote retweets simply stating 'same'. Which, while carrying concerning suggestions about how much some of the bot's followers drink, is also comforting, for we can rest assured that Twitter is in fact usable by those in the afterlife.

Margery Golde died on 22 June in 1297, in Oxford – the city of terrible clerks. While I can't be sure where exactly her house was situated, I do know she lived within the parish of St Peter-in-the-East, a twelfth-century church which still exists in Oxford today.[*] The tavern she had been drinking at

---

[*] It is now the St Edmund Hall library on Queen's Lane, north of the High Street in central Oxford.

that night with her husband is unnamed in her inquest, but we can imagine it was somewhere close enough to be able to get extremely drunk and then stumble home safely – markedly *without* falling into a ditch and dying.[*]

Having made it home, escaping the perils of ditches in the night, Margery 'fixed a lighted candle on the wall' by the bed she shared with her husband. The couple then got into bed 'and left the candle burning and immediately fell asleep; and when the candle had burnt as far as the wall, that which remained fell on the straw by their bed, and burnt it and the said Margery even to the belly, whereof she died on the next day, but she had all church rites'.

If there was ever a PSA to not drink and light candles, it sure seems like this would be it.

But in all fairness, while alcohol certainly plays a role in Margery's death, the real culprit is the straw, or rushes, laid out over the floor. A century later in Bedfordshire, Alice Saddler left her house on an errand, and in closing the door, created a draft that spread the fire from the hearth to the straw on the floor and burned the house down.[1] John of Norfolk, a fifty-year-old chaplain also (probably) from Bedfordshire,[†] burned down his rectory when a candle he forgot to extinguish fell down upon the straw over the floor.

---

[*] This is likely due to the time of year – if Margery heeded the town curfew, there may have been light yet in the sky to help her navigate around danger.

[†] I was unable to access the source for this death myself, but I *believe* it to be from Bedfordshire in the late fourteenth century.

While covering the floor of one's home with a highly flammable material may seem unwise, there was good reason for it. Many floors of the era, especially those of the lower classes, were clay, which not only held on to cold, but damp as well. A covering of straw offered protection from this damp and cold, and even provided a small amount of cushion. It proved to be such a popular and affordable treatment in homes – even in greater halls that may have had cobbled or flagstone floors – that the trend in England endured from Margery's time up until that of the great Humanist philosopher Erasmus. And we know this because during his stay in England, he complained about it. Vividly:

> *The floors [in England]... are generally spread with clay and then with rushes from some marsh, which are renewed from time to time but so as to leave a basic layer, sometimes for twenty years, under which fester spittle, vomit, dogs' urine and men's too, dregs of beer and cast-off bits of fish, and other unspeakable kinds of filth. As the weather changes, this exhales a sort of miasma which in my opinion is far from conducive to bodily health.*[*]

---

[*] From a letter to John Francis, physician to the Cardinal of York, dating 1524. I would like to note, as well, that I originally found a much 'nicer' translated copy of this letter, which omitted 'vomit' and did not add that the urine was of men as well as dogs.

So the trade-off for a warm, cushioned floor for cheap was... *this*. Of course, we must take Erasmus' letter with a grain of salt, as it may have been written from an uncharitable point of view.[*] But the one important thing this letters shows us is that stinking, straw-strewn floors are not a medieval myth, unlike heavily spiced rotten meat and whatever other nonsense you might read on a listicle site that exists solely for garnering advertising revenue. People of the Middle Ages, and even up through the Renaissance, covered the floors of their homes with old straw or rushes – sometimes scenting them with sweet herbs – and sometimes what lurked beneath was abhorrently foul. In the television series *Secrets of the Castle*, which takes a look at the construction in France of a twelfth-century castle using historic methods, Ruth Goodman hypothesises that the lower level of straw may have been left to 'compost', as it were, which certainly could account for a smell, and is supported by what we read from Erasmus.

Just *how* rushes or straw was laid out over the floor is unknown. Goodman, in the aforementioned series, hypothesises that rushes or straw may have been not strewn about loosely on the floor, but kept in small bound bundles and arranged in a sort of herringbone pattern. You can think of it as being in the same spirit as braided rugs made of old scraps of fabric, but without having been sewn together. This laying

---

[*] I could not definitely find much about Erasmus' relationship with England as a whole, though it does seem like he spent his entire time at Queens' College in Cambridge complaining.

pattern would have kept it tidy and underfoot, and perhaps even sweepable, if it was bound tightly enough. However, we really don't know how they were laid out.

The sinister candle 'fixed on the wall' is much easier to place and envision than the straw floor covering. The candle would have been spiked upon a bit of iron in the wall, preventing the need for an oil lamp (which they certainly used in the Middle Ages), or any sort of candlestick holder.

And there you have it: an easy medieval recipe for burning to death in your sleep. Lots of alcohol to start (just for flavour, really), paired with a single flame that drops to the ground and lights the rushes on fire. It travels over the ground to the bed where it engulfs those within in flames.

And so Margery Golde, drunk beyond measure, was burned in her sleep even to the belly, and died the next day. Adam, her husband, 'scarce escaped his own death', having 'his hands and feet... burnt to the bones, so that scarce he will recover'.

As grim as Margery's death and the ailments of her husband may have been, it's not the worst house fire on record. Another couple had a similar night in 1326: Alice Ryvet and her husband John were woken at midnight by a fire which had been caused by the fall of the lighted candle as they were going to sleep. Alice and John both escaped, but when John discovered that his wife was to blame for the fire, he was so incensed that he pushed her back into the flames and fled. Alice, badly burned, died a week later.

10

LOITERING WITH THIRTEEN COMPANIONS

The Death of Reginald de Freestone

from Calendar of Coroners Rolls of the City of London

t is sometime around midnight on 2 February 1322 in the great city of London, and Reginald de Freestone is having the time of his life. Or, well… we would hope he was, given that this is his last night on this earth. After the curtains of curfew have been closed, Reginald, along with his mates John 'Bocche',* Walter le Skynnere and 'eleven others whose names are unknown', take to revelling down Bradstrete, 'singing and shouting as they often did at night'.

This doesn't go down well with the residents of Bradstrete. William de 'Grymsyby',† a shopkeeper, is awoken by the noise and beseeches Reginald and his companions to allow him and his neighbours to sleep and rest in peace. Reginald and his

---

* Also spelled 'Becche' in the inquest.
† Quotes original to inquest.

company of thirteen other men do no such thing, and instead invite William to 'come out of his shop if he [dares]'.

Take a moment to imagine the scene: it's a dark, cold, winter night on a narrow, medieval street, the timber buildings that line it leaning over the cobblestones, allowing only a band of starry sky to be seen above. Reginald de Freestone, an arrowhead maker,[*] is leading a group of thirteen men, all or most of whom are belting out songs, scattered with jubilant shouting, their drunken breath puffing cold in the night. Above, a light appears in a window and the man bearing it shouts down at them to *please* shut the fuck up because people are trying to sleep. This is *not* the time for singing. Reginald, emboldened by drink and the spirit of the night, doesn't want to stop. We can imagine a sparkle of delight in Reginald's eyes as he detects a possible altercation – the one thing that might turn a good night into an even better story. So he shouts up to the shopkeeper, William, that he can come down if he likes.

What he is not expecting is for William to come out of his shop brandishing 'a staff called "Balstaf". Nor, do I think, is he expecting the man to run at him – which he does. Reginald must not have taken it very seriously, or perhaps wasn't much of a runner himself, for William catches up with him and smites 'the said Reginald with the staff on the left side of the head', smashing 'the whole of his head therewith, so that he fell to the ground'.

---

[*] Also known as a 'settere', which is what the original inquest calls him.

So much for a good night.

Reginald lies there, at the entrance of the tenement of Jordan de 'Langeleye', unable to speak, until the break of day. He then dies.

William himself flees after Reginald's death, 'but whither he went and who harboured him they know not', which means William probably got away with this little bit of murder. Not that it was all roses for William afterward, as his crime meant he had to give up all his chattels, which are handily listed in the inquest as being: two pigs, a 'shippingboard', a broken chest, a table, one pair of worn linen sheets, a blanket, a worn linen cloth, and 'other small things' worth 2s. 9½d.

The most interesting thing about Reginald's death, however, is not the mysterious unnamed thirteen companions, nor is it William's 'Balstaf', but the simple fact that it takes place in London. Which means the location is traceable – but where in the world is Bradstrete?

Thankfully for me, I like digging around old maps and scouring books for documents and first-hand accounts that might mention contemporary street names, because Reginald's death took a *ton* of it.

The inquest states that the group of revellers is on 'the street called Bradstrete, near the gate of the tenement held by Juliana de Bromford of Jordan de 'Langeleye' in the parish of St Peter de

---

* Also spelled 'Langelegh' in the inquest.

Bradstrete'. Unfortunately for us, Julia de Bromford and Jordan de 'Langeleye' seem to have left no record of their tenement, so their gate is useless to us. The parish of St Peter de 'Bradstrete' also seems to have disappeared. The only lead is one lone mention of Bradstrete as the location of the guild hall acquired by the Merchant Taylors in 1392, some seventy years after Reginald's death. Luckily for us, the location, if not the original building of the Merchant Taylors' Hall, still exists in London today. But it's not on 'Bradstrete' – it's on Threadneedle Street. And it's not in the ward of St Peter de 'Bradstrete', but Cornhill.

Turns out, Threadneedle Street got its name somewhere around 1598. Before that, it was part of *Broad* Street. Aha! 'Bradstrete', then, is one of those curious medieval spellings owing to accent or personal preference.[*]

If we consult the Agas map of London from 1578, we can see 'Brode Street' clearly labelled on what corresponds to what is now Old Broad Street. It dead ends, not at Liverpool Street station as it does today, but at the south-eastern corner of the All Hallows churchyard,[†] the church itself being situated on the London Wall.

While Old Broad Street is now in the ward of Cornhill, it wasn't always so. The events of 2 February happen in the ward

---

[*] The lack of standardised spelling in the era, as well as the Great Vowel Shift, is likely why 'Broadstreet' is repeatedly spelled 'Bradstrete' throughout the inquest.

[†] The Agas map spells this as "All Haloues in y Wall". This church should not be confused with the All Hallows on Bread Street, Lombard Street, All Hallows Barking, All Hallows Staining, All Hallows the Great or All Hallows the Less.

of 'Bradstrete', and mentions 'Cornhulle' being a neighbouring ward from which jurors for the inquest were summoned. In John Stow's *Survey of London*, conducted in 1598 and published in 1603, he describes the 'Brodeſtreete warde' as a somewhat triangular-shaped ward between Brode Street, Moorsgate and the Stocks Market. At some point in time, however, this ward seems to have been absorbed into Cornhill, as Old Broad Street and Threadneedle Street occupy this ward in modern-day London.

With that said, I'm quite comfortable placing Reginald's death somewhere on Old Broad Street or Threadneedle Street. And given that in 1322, the northern end of Old Broad Street terminated at the London Wall, this means Reginald died somewhere on a stretch of road only about half a mile long.

So beware, any revellers, of this stretch of road on cold, February nights. Be quiet, and let people sleep, lest you be taken to your maker by an angry shopkeeper with a Balstaf.

11

A FOUR-AND-A-HALF-FOOT SWORD

The Death of William Castle

from *Select Cases from the Coroners' Rolls, A.D. 1265–1413*

s a final treat, here is the case of William Castle and the four-and-a-half-foot sword. The inquest is a twisting jewel of a report, and so I present it here in its unadulterated entirety, exactly as it reads in translation from *Select Cases from the Coroners' Rolls*. It is not the longest inquest from the books I've sourced for *Unfortunate Ends*, but it is the one with the biggest sword. I do hope you enjoy reading it – and trying to make sense of it!

At the county court of Northampton held on Thursday next before the feast of St Barnabas the Apostle in the fifth year of King Edward, Margaret, formerly the wife of William Castle of Barnwell near Oundle, finds pledges to prosecute her appeal against John Blogwine of Oundle for the death of the said William, formerly her husband, to wit, John Porthors of Polebrook and Robert of Sutton of Barnwell; and forthwith she appeals the said John in the following words.

Margaret, formerly the wife of William Castle of Barnwell near Oundle, who is here, appeals John Blogwine of Oundle for the death of the said William Castle of Barnwell near Oundle, formerly her husband, who was killed in her arms, for that on Monday of Whitsun week at the hour of vespers in May in the fifth year of our lord King Edward, who now reigns (God guard him), while Margaret and the said William Castle of Barnwell near Oundle, formerly her husband, were in the peace of God and of our lord King Edward, who now reigns (God guard him), in the vill of Oundle in Northamptonshire, on an arch on the west side of a bridge called in English Crowthorp bridge, which is built of stone and mortar, and crosses the river Nen from Oundle on the north to Crowthorp on the south (the width of the bridge is twelve feet between the two crosses which stand upon it, and it extends twenty feet from one cross towards the north and forty feet from the other cross towards the south), John Blogwine of Oundle came there *on the said bridge, at the said hour of the said day and year, feloniously and as a felon of our lord the king and against the king's peace, his crown and his dignity, almost joining body to body in await [lying in wait] and with premeditated assault, and he assaulted the said William Castle of Barnwell near Oundle, formerly the husband of the said Margaret, feloniously and as a felon of our lord the king, and struck the said William Castle of Barnwell near Oundle, formerly her husband, feloniously and as a felon of our lord the king, with a polished sword of iron and steel. Its length was four feet and a half; its width near the hilt was three inches and a half, in the centre three inches, and at the end one inch;* the blade was of iron and steel intermixed, the hilt and the pommel were of well-polished iron, and the handle was of iron bound and fetted with iron threads. And with that sword, while she held [William] in her arms, [John] gave him a mortal wound on the left leg five inches from the knee; the wound was eight inches long, four inches wide, and four inches deep, extending through the brawn to the bone, so that if there had been no other wound*

---

* This is an incredibly large sword for the era, no matter what video games will have you believe. Most medieval swords have a blade length of roughly thirty inches and were two inches wide at the hilt, and come in weighing about 2 lbs.

or blow, he would have died of that wound. Thus of that very wound the said William Castle of Barnwell near Oundle, formerly the husband of the said Margaret, died in her arms at sunset of the said day. This felony the said John Blogwine of Oundle committed feloniously and as a felon of our lord the king against his peace, his crown, and his dignity. And after causing this death and doing this felony feloniously and as a felon of our lord the king, he fled forthwith. And the said Margaret, who was the wife of William Castle of Barnwell near Oundle and who is there, at once at the said hour of the said day and year and at the aforesaid place raised the hue and cry against the said John Blogwine of Oundle, as against a felon of our lord the king, and she at once made suit from vill to vill to the four neighbouring vills, and so to the bailiffs of our lord the king, and from the bailiffs to the coroners, and so to the next county court, which is now [being held]. And if the said John Blogwine of Oundle will deny this death and this felony, the said Margaret, formerly the wife of the said William, who is here, is ready to prove it, in such wise as the court considers that as a woman she ought to prove it against a man.

At the county court of Northamptonshire held on Thursday [6 July 1312] the eve of the Translation of St Thomas the Martyr at the end of the said year, Margaret prosecuted her appeal against John Blogwine of Oundle, who was exacted for the first time, but did not appear.

And at the second county court of Northampton held on Thursday [3 August 1312] next after the feast of St Peter's Chains at the beginning of the sixth year of King Edward, Margaret prosecuted her appeal against John Blogwine of Oundle, who was exacted the second time, but did not appear.

And at the third county court of Northampton held on Thursday [31 August 1312] next after the feast of the Beheading of St John the Baptist in the said year, Margaret prosecuted her appeal against John Blogwine of Oundle, who was exacted the third time, but did not appear.

And at the fourth county court of Northampton held on Thursday [28 September 1312] the eve of Michaelmas in the said year, Margaret prosecuted her appeal against John Blogwine of Oundle, who was exacted the fourth time and did not appear, but he was mainprised* by William Baxter of Oundle.

---

* Mainprise is basically bail.

And at the fifth county court of Northampton held on Thursday [26 October 1312] next before the feast of the Apostles Simon and Jude in the said year, Margaret prosecuted her appeal against John Blogwine of Oundle. And a writ of the king was received removing the appeal [from the county court], as hereafter appears.

Edward by the grace of God, etc. to the sheriff of Northampton greeting. We order you to cause the appeal which Margaret, formerly the wife of William Castle of Barnwell near Oundle, is making in your county court against John Blogwine of Oundle, Walter of Castor, John Papillon of Oundle, and Nicholas Aketoner of Oundle, for the death of the said William, formerly her husband, to come before our justices at Westminster on the morrow of St Martin [12 November 1312] with the attachments and all other adminicles* touching that appeal, and tell Margaret that then and there she is to prosecute her appeal against the said John, Walter, John, and Nicholas, if she wishes. And have this writ there. Witness myself at Windsor the fifteenth day of October in the sixth year of our reign. For the said appeal cannot be terminated according to the

---

* Proof and/or witnesses.

*law and custom of our realm in any lower court,
but only before us or elsewhere before our justices.
Let this writ be executed if the said John, Walter,
John, and Nicholas request it, and not otherwise.*

*And hence nothing more was done in the
said appeal.*

NOTES

Chapter 1: The Innocent Clerk

1 Paul W. Knoll, '*Nationes* and Other Bonding Groups at Late Medieval Central European Universities', *Mobs: An Interdisciplinary Inquiry*, edited by Nancy van Deusen and Leonard Michael Koff, Leiden and Boston, Brill, 2012, p. 96.

2 Scott Jenkins, 'War War War! Slay the Welsh Dogs!', *The Medieval Student*, at https://themedievalstudent. wordpress.com/2012/05/06/war-war-war-slay-slay-slay-the-welsh-dogs/

Chapter 2: A Trail of Blood

1 William Chester Jordan, 'A Fresh Look at Medieval Sanctuary', *Law and the Illicit in Medieval Europe*, 2008, p. 18.

2 *Calendar of Coroners Rolls of the City of London*, p. xviii.

Chapter 3: John Wick Goes Medieval

1 Edward of Norwich, *The Master of Game*, edited by William Adolph and Florence Baillie-Grohman, London, Chatto & Windus, 1909, pp. 80–82.

2 MS Bodley 764, translated by Richard Barber.

Chapter 4: Foul Tredekeiles

1 Frances Gies and Joseph Gies, *Women in the Middle Ages*, New York, Barnes & Noble, 1980, p. 41.

2 Ibid., p. 52.

Chapter 5: The Penetrated Fundament

1 Barbara A. Hanawalt, *The Ties That Bound*, New York, Oxford University Press, 1986, p. 274.

2 Ibid., p. 132.

3 'the majority of homicides occurred in village fields (59 percent), particularly during plowing or harvest, when competition for crops was at its keenest in peasant communities.' (Ibid., p. 23.)

Chapter 7: The Sow Was Arrested

1 '28 If a bull gores a man or woman to death, the bull is to be stoned to death, and its meat must not be eaten. But the owner of the bull will not be held responsible. 29 If, however, the bull has had the habit of goring and the owner has been warned but has not kept it penned up and it kills a man or woman, the bull is to be stoned and its owner also is to be put to death.' Exodus 21:28–29.

2 Piers Biernes, 'The Law is an Ass', *Society & Animals*, 1995, p. 29.

3 E. P. Evans, *The Criminal Prosecution and Capital Punishment of Animals*, London, W. Heinemann, 1906, p. 138.

4   *Records of Medieval Oxford*, p. 46.

5   Barbara A. Hanawalt, *The Ties That Bound*, New York, Oxford University Press, 1986, p. 175.

6   Ibid., p. 177.

Chapter 8: A Pit Full of Shit

1   Henry Ellis et al., *Monasticon Anglicanum*, London, T. G. March, 1849, p. 249.

2   Jonathan Sharpe, 'Oseney Abbey, Oxford: Archaeological Investigations, 1975–1983', *Oxoniensia*, p. 99.

3   David Roffe and Christine Roffe, 'Madness and Care in the Community: A Medieval Perspective', *BMJ*, 1995.

Chapter 9: Drunk Beyond Measure

1   Barbara A. Hanawalt, *The Ties That Bound*, New York, Oxford University Press, 1986, p. 37.

BIBLIOGRAPHY

Ackermann, Rudolph, *A History of the University of Oxford, Its Colleges, Halls, and Public Buildings: In Two Volumes*, London, Harrison, 1814.

Agas, Ralph, *The Agas Map*, 1578, https://mapoflondon.uvic.ca/agas.htm

Aston, T. H., et al., *The History of the University of Oxford: The Early Oxford Schools*, India, Clarendon Press, 1984.

Bayley, Justine, and Egan, Geoff, *The Medieval Household: Daily Living, c. 1150–c. 1450.* 2nd ed., Woodbridge, Boydell Press, 2010.

Beirnes, Piers, 'The Law is an Ass: Reading E. P. Evans', *The Medieval Prosecution and Capital Punishment of Animals*', *Society & Animals*, vol. 2, issue 1, 1995, pp. 27–46.

Bestiary: Being an English Version of the Bodleian Library, Oxford, MS Bodley 764, translated by Richard Barber, Woodbridge, Boydell Press, 1992.

Blaeu, Joan, *Bedfordiensis comitatus; anglis Bedford Shire*, Old Maps Online, http://www.oldmapsonline.org/map/unibern/000993855

Brears, Peter, *Cooking & Dining in Medieval England*, Totnes, Prospect Books, 2008.

Calendar of Coroners Rolls of the City of London A.D. 1300–1378, edited by Reginald R. Sharpe, London, Richard Clay and Sons, Ltd., 1908.

Carson, Hampton L., 'The Trial of Animals and Insects. A Little Known Chapter of Mediæval Jurisprudence', *Proceedings of the American Philosophical Society*, vol. 56, no. 5, 1917, pp. 410–415, *JSTOR*, www.jstor.org/stable/984029

Ellis, Henry, et al., *Monasticon Anglicanum: A History of the Abbies and Other Monasteries, Hospitals, Frieries, and Cathedral and Collegiate Churches, with Their Dependencies, in England and Wales.* Originally Published in Latin, London, T. G. March, 1849.

Erasmus, Desiderius, *The Correspondence of Erasmus: Letters 1356 to 1534, 1523 to 1524*, Toronto and London, University of Toronto Press, 1974.

Evans, E. P., *The Criminal Prosecution and Capital Punishment of Animals*, London, W. Heinemann, 1906.

Finkelstein, J. J., 'The Ox That Gored', *Transactions of the American Philosophical Society*, vol. 71, no. 2, 1981, pp. 1–89, *JSTOR*, www.jstor.org/stable/1006346

Geggel, Laura, 'Rare tile of mythical beast discovered in 14th-century cesspit', *LiveScience*, 5 March 2020, www.livescience.com/english-cesspit-artifacts.html

Gies, Frances, and Gies, Joseph, *Life in a Medieval Village*, New York, HarperPerrenial, 1991.

—. *Marriage and Family in the Middle Ages*, 1987, New York, Harper & Row, 1989.

—. *Women in the Middle Ages*, New York, Barnes & Noble, 1980.

Green, Thomas A., 'The Jury and the English Law of Homicide, 1200–1600', University of Michigan Law School Scholarship Repository, repository.law.umich.edu/cgi/viewcontent.cgi?article=1136&context=articles

Grundhauser, Eric, 'What It Was Like to Seek Asylum in Medieval England', *Slate*, 13 July 2015, https://slate.com/human-interest/2015/07/in-medieval-england-fugitives-seeking-sanctuary-needed-only-to-get-themselves-to-church.html

Hanawalt, Barbara A., *The Ties That Bound*, New York, Oxford University Press, 1986.

—. 'Childrearing among the Lower Classes of Late Medieval England', *The Journal of Interdisciplinary History*, vol. 8, no. 1, 1977, pp. 1–22, *JSTOR*, www.jstor.org/stable/202593

Henley, Walter of, *Walter of Henley's Husbandry*, translated by Elizabeth Lamond, London, New York, Longmans Green and Co., 1890.

'Houses of Augustinian canons: The abbey of Oseney', *A History of the County of Oxford: Volume 2*, edited by William Page, London, Victoria County History, 1907, pp. 90–93, *British History Online*, http://www.british-history.ac.uk/vch/oxon/vol2/

Jenkins, Scott, 'War War War, Slay Slay Slay the Welsh Dogs!', *The Medieval Student*, 6 May 2012, https://themedievalstudent.wordpress.com/2012/05/06/war-war-war-slay-slay-slay-the-welsh-dogs/

Jenkins, Stephanie, '106: *Vacant* & 107: A-Plan Insurance', *Oxford History: The High*, http://www.oxfordhistory.org.uk/high/tour/south/106_107.html.

Jones, Richard, 'Manure and the Medieval Social Order', *Medievalists.net*, March 2013, www.medievalists.net/2013/03/manure-and-the-medieval-social-order/

Jordan, William Chester, 'A Fresh Look at Medieval Sanctuary', in *Law and the Illicit in Medieval Europe*, edited by Ruth Mazo Karras, Joel Kaye and E. Ann Matter, Philadelphia, University of Pennsylvania Press, 2008, pp. 17–32.

Kerr, Julie, *Life in the Medieval Cloister*, New York, Continuum, 2009.

Knoll, Paul W., '*Nationes* and Other Bonding Groups at Late Medieval Central European Universities', in *Mobs: An Interdisciplinary Inquiry*, edited by Nancy van Deusen and Leonard Michael Koff, Leiden and Boston, Brill, 2012, pp. 95–115.

Lillich, Meredith Parsons, 'Cleanliness with Godliness: A Discussion of Medieval Monastic Plumbing', *Mélanges à la Mémoire du Père Anselme Dimier*, edited by B. Chauvin, vol. 5, pp. 123–149, academia.edu/36423701/_Cleanliness_with_Godliness_A_Discussion_of_Medievl_Monastic_Plumbing_

Luttrell Psalter, BL Add. MS 42130.

'Medieval Traffic Problems', *Medievalists.net, Middle English Dictionary,* Regents of the University of Michigan, 2019, https://quod.lib.umich.edu/m/middle-english-dictionary/dictionary

Mortimer, Ian, *The Time Traveller's Guide to Medieval England,* London, Vintage, 2009.

Norwich, Edward of, *The Master of Game,* edited by William Adolph and Florence Baillie-Grohman, London, Chatto & Windus, 1909.

Oakeshott, Ewart, *Records of the Medieval Sword,* Woodbridge, The Boydell Press, 1991.

Pearl, Kibre, 'The Nations in the Medieval Universities', *The American Historical Review,* vol 54, issue 3, April 1949, p. 572, https://doi.org/10.1086/ahr/54.3.572

Rannie, David Watson, *Oriel College (Oxford University),* London, F. E. Robinson & Company, 1900.

Records of the Borough of Leicester, edited by Mary Bateson, London, Cambridge University Press Warehouse, 1899.

Records of Medieval Oxford, edited by H. E. Salter, Oxford, The Oxford Chronicle Company, Ltd. 1912.

Reeves, Compton, *Pleasures and Pastimes in Medieval England*, Stroud, Alan Sutton Publishing Limited, 1995.

Roffe, David, and Roffe, Christine, 'Madness and care in the community: a medieval perspective', *BMJ*, 23 December 1995.

Select Cases from the Coroners' Rolls A.D. 1265–1413, London, Selden Society, 1896.

Sharpe, Jonathan, 'Oseney Abbey, Oxford: Archaeological Investigations, 1975–1983', *Oxoniensia*, vol. 50, 1885, pp. 95–130, oxoniensia.org/volumes/1985/sharpe.pdf

'Sterquilinus', Wikipedia, Wikimedia Foundation, 10 August 2020, en.wikipedia.org/wiki/Sterquilinus

'St Mary Spital Cemetery', edited by Maryanne Kowaleski, *Medieval London*, 2017, medievallondon.ace.fordham.edu/exhibits/show/medieval-london-sites/stmaryspitalcemetery

'St Peter-in-the-East', Wikipedia, Wikimedia Foundation, 30 June 2020, en.wikipedia.org/wiki/St_Peter-in-the-East

'St Peter upon Cornhill', The Worshipful Company of Parish Clerks, *London Parish Clerks*, 2015, londonparishclerks. smugmug.com/Parishes-Churches/Individual-Parish-Info/St-Peter-upon-Cornhill

Thornbury, Walter, 'Threadneedle Street', *Old and New London: Volume 1*, London, Cassell, Petter & Galpin, 1878, pp. 531–544, *British History Online*, 22 January 2021, http://www. british-history.ac.uk/old-new-london/vol1/pp531-544

Trenery, Claire, and Horden, Peregrine, 'Madness in the Middle Ages', *The Routledge History of Madness and Mental Health*, www.routedgehandbooks/com/doi/10.4324/9781315202211.ch3

'Catte Street', Wikipedia, Wikimedia Foundation, 18 May 2021, en.wikipedia.org/wiki/Catte_Street

'University Church of St Mary the Virgin', Wikipedia, Wikimedia Foundation, 6 March 2022, en.wikipedia.org/wiki/ University_Church_of_St_Mary_the_Virgin

Wood, Anthony à, and Claerk, Andrew, *Survey of the Antiquities of the City of Oxford, composed in 1661–6, by Anthony Wood*, Oxford, Clarendon Press, 1889.

Supporters

Unbound is the world's first crowdfunding publisher, established in 2011.

We believe that wonderful things can happen when you clear a path for people who share a passion. That's why we've built a platform that brings together readers and authors to crowdfund books they believe in – and give fresh ideas that don't fit the traditional mould the chance they deserve.

This book is in your hands because readers made it possible. Everyone who pledged their support is listed below. Join them by visiting unbound.com and supporting a book today.

Lucinda Abbott

Marion Kiser Adam

Geoff Adams

Keith Adams

Kelsey Adelson

Dan Alban

Douglas Alexander

Syeda Ali

Ashley Allen

Kathryn Allen

Shelley Allen

Grady Alsabrook

Alexis Alvarez

Jamie Anderson

Kris Anderson

Sydney Anderson

Bernard Angell

Christian Ankerstjerne

Kirk Annett

Amanda Appleby

Barry Archer

Sharon Aris

Steven Arnott

Liz Artemis

Sabrina Artus

Sophia Asbury

Adrian Ashton

Arshaad Asruf

Martyn Atkins

William Atkins

Tom Atkinson

Marcus Austin

Simon Austin

Johan B Eriksson

Clay Baker

Jeff Baker

Ray Baldry

Radley Balko

Lori Baluta

Alex Banks

Miroslaw Baran

Clare Barker

Ann and Howard Barlow

Karen Barlow

Jessica L. Barnes

Michael Barnes

Grace Barrett

Bob Barringer

Laura Bartlett

Steve Bass

Andrew Bateman

Andrew Batten

John Baughman

Vikki Bayman

Betsy Bearden

Elzbieta Beck

Jane "Superplum" Bedwell

Patrick Benetz

Issy Benson

Keren Berkovitz

Courtney Bermack

Jenn Biddle

Will Biel

J. Kyle Bienvenu

April Bingham

Jane Black

Laura Blackwell

Amy Blair

Nicholas Blair

Deb Blakley Rasmussen

Amy Louise Blaney

Graham Blenkin

Lee Boal

Chris Bodem

Ali Bodin

David Bofinger

Anne Bogart

DJ Booker

Terry Bosky

Gareth Bouch

Maggi Boult

Paige Bowelle

Linda Bowser

Lydia Boyko

Richard W H Bray

Robin Bray

Karen Brenchley

Geoffrey and Gillian Brent

Wendy Breyer

Katie Bridger

Stacy Bright

Andrea Brin

Alice Broadribb

Gregory Brockman

Jess Brooks

Emma M. Brown

Margaret JC Brown

Brian Browne

Christopher Buecheler

Emma Bull

Anwen Bullen

Matt Bunker

Rob Burch

Kimberly D Burke

Joseph Burne

Dr Victoria J Burton

Kay Buttfield

Sandra Buttigieg

Kit Byatt

Lily C.

Elizabeth Cady

Emily Cain

Regina Caldart

Sarah Camino

Aeroferret Campana

Elizabeth Campbell

Floyd Canfield

Marianna Caparelli

Stevie Carroll

Victoria Carroll

Ciarán Carter

Chris Chafin

Ranjit Chagar

Rachael Chappell

KJ Charles

Scott Chaussee

Paul Child

Jacob Childress

Nathan Chinchen

Johnny Chiodini

Alexander Chreky

William Christensen

Anthony Christopher

Don Church

Carl Clare

Dwayne Clare

Thomas Claringbold

Simon Clark

Perry Clarke

Tom Clarke

Ian Clarkson

Mary Cleaton

Alex Clements

Rebecca Cloonan

Jeremy Coffey

Scott Cohan

Kathryn Coll

Gina Collia

Philip Collins

Alexe Colvin

Heather Combe

Amelia Cooper

Mark E Cooper

Richard Cooper

Joshua Coppard

Copysquirl

Amy Cormier

Bill Cornell

Robert Corr

Adri Cortesia

Mark Cotter

Leigh Cotterill

Aoife Cragg

Derek Cramer

Julie Cramer

John Crawford

Kim Crawford

Anthony Creagh

Emma Creasey

Alistair Crooks

Simon Cross

CrystalLakeManagment

Heather Cunningham

Melissa Cunningham

James Curtis

Craig Czyz

J D

Emily Dagger

Patricia Daloni

Sarah Dalrymple

Louise Starkowsky Dancause

Paula Davidson

Sue Davies

E R Andrew Davis

Emily Davis

Kenneth Davis

Kate Dawson

DB

Nishantha de Alwis

Angela Dean

Michael Dean

Death by boredom

Diana DeFrancesco

Eno Deka

Clémence Deleuze

Jonathan Denny

Pete Dewhirst

Christopher DiBona (clerk)

Alyson Dickerman

Stephanie Dickinson

Tim Dierks

Caroline Diezyn

Joe Ding

Andrew Disney

Dana DiTomaso

Rob Dobry

Jennifer Dodgson

Kayleigh Doherty

Christine Donlan

Kevin Donnellon

Nik Doran

Rae Douglass

John Dovey

Bethan Downing

Cressida Downing

Jeremy Doyel

David Drinkwater

Katy Driver

Jackie Duckworth

Ole-Morten Duesund

Hannah Duggan

John David Duke Jr

Christyn Dundorf

Wendi Dunlap

Aaron Dunn

Ryan Dunn

Sheila Dunn

Steve Dunn

Timothy Dunn

Emma Durocher

Jennifer Dury

James Duyck

Maeve Dwyer

Thom Dyke

Chris Eagle

Robert Eardley

Alice Ebenhoe

Hugh Eckert

Gillian Edwards

Eamonn Egginton

Ira Ehrlich

Carol Eicher

Janice Eisen

Thérèse Elaine

Robert Eliason

Richard Ellis

Hilary Emmons

William English

M Etherton

Dennis Evanosky

Cath Evans

Adam Everett

Jackson Ewing

Bad ExampleMan

Sharon Eyre

M. J. Fahy

Jennie Faries

Louise Farquharson

Nic Farra

Katie Faulk

Cariston Fawcett

Nicole Featherby

Charlotte Featherstone

Dorothy Ferguson

Robert Ferguson

David Fernandez

Annie Fields

Joshua Fields

August Fietkau

Laura Filipchuk

Robert Finch

Jennie Findlay

David Finlay

Susan Fino

Stephen Fishbach

Ashley Fisher

Alex Flinsch

Philip Flint

Jason Folkman

Lila Fontes

For RF

William Forsyth

Jeremy Francis

Edward Freedman

Peter Freese

Lincoln Freimund

Mr & Mrs Frennall

Marsha Friedrich

Brenda Fry

John Fry

Deborah Fulmer

Rodney Funk

Matthew Gagle

Todd Galle

Neil Garland

Michael Gates

Jo Gatford

Deborah Gatty

Lia Gelder

Richard Gidwaney

Maggie Gilbert

Julie Giles

Andrea Gill

Michael Glass

Shannon Glazer

Paulo Glórias

Amy Godliman

Annette Goeres

Dennis Gokman

Meaghan Good

Pat Gower

Timothy H. Gray

Bethany Green

Emi Green

Karen Green

Tony Greengrass

Trisha Greenstone

Autumn Greer

Eamonn Griffin

Katie Griffiths

Mike Griffiths

James Grimmelmann

Lynn Grindall

Lacy Grove

Mark Groves

Angela Gunn

Johanna Haban

Emma Håkonsen

Cris Hale

Jon Hall

Matthew Hall

Chris Halliday

Halo Café Celbridge

Meg Halstead

Theodora Hamburg

Russell Hamm

Stephen Hampshire

Lynn Haney III

Jeremy Hanks

Catherine Hanley

Donna Hanson

Brandon Hardin

Marianne Harding

Julie Hardy

Tim Hardy

Matthew Harffy

Pat Harkin

Philip Harkins

Melissa Harkness

Sean Harmeyer

J Harris

Jess Harris

Heidi Hart

Joan Hartley

Lars Hasvoll Bakke

Melinda Haunton

Emma Hawes

Stuart Hawkes

Sophie Hazlewood

Paul Hazlitt

Jodi Head

Spencer Healey

Jayne Heathcock

Paula Heathwaite

Lindsey Henderson

Douglas Henke

Jo Henn

Laura Henson

Lucy Henzell-Thomas

Maureen Heon

Kevin Heywood

Benjamin G Higson

Janosch Hildebrand

Robin Hill

Catherine Hills

Lisa Hirsch

Philip Hirst

Michael Hobson

Vincent Hodges

Kevin Aston Hoey

Niall Holden

Jason Holland

James Holloway

Damian Holter

Bob Honey

Geoffrey Horn

Steve Horner

Simon Horspool

Robert Horvath

Katy Hoskyn

Samantha Hourston-Quirk

Charlie Housley

Robert Howatson

Sam Howe

Steven Howell

Matt Huggins

Brianne Hughes

Kevin Hughes

Tom Hughes

Jay Humphrey

Sam Humphries

Andrew Huntley

Jessica Hurtgen

K.R. Ilves

Martyn Ingram

Nathan Irvin

Neil Irving

Tim Irving

Marc W Jasper

Jax

Mike Jenkins

Mary Jennings

Jenny

Brett Jensen

Robin Jervis

Colin Johnson

James Johnson

Mark Johnson

Victoria Johnston

Harriet Jones

Hugh Jones

Julie Iler Jones

Karen Jones

Lauren Jones

Phyl Jones

Tim Jones

Mathew Jose

Phoebe Juel

Laura Juliff

Gary Kacmarcik

Rachael Kane

Josh Kanto

John Kaye

Lizzie Kaye

Seamus Keane

Matthew Keck

Scott Keever

Dorian Kelley

Craig Kellner

Helen Kemp

Val Kemp

Ian Kendall

Martin Kennedy

Alex Kenney

Jacob Kesinger

Dan Kieran

Robert Killian

Anne Kinderlerer

Alan King

Manuela Kipper

Hannah Klevesahl

Candace Kochosky

Jim Kokocki

John Koshy

Ryan Kovar

Sydney Kovar

Abby Kraft

Matthew Kremske

Greg Krohn

Matthijs Krul

Denise Kruse (clerk)

Bob Kuhn

Keith Kurtz

Seren L.

Karin L.Kross

Pierre L'Allier

Morgan L'Fey

Edith Laird

Anne Lamb

Anna Lanners

Nick Lansing

Clifford Lauri

Kerry Lavin-Thomson

Robert Law

Kyle Lawcock

Janet Lawrence

Sarah Laws

Bryan Lawson

Jamie Lear

Darcy Leidolph

Daniel Lemmon

Eugene Leonard

Maria Leván

Karin Lewicki

Briannah lewis

David Lewis

Duncan Lewis

Tim Lewis

Megann Licskai

Jennifer Liechty Douglas

Jonathan Light

Tristan Linck

Ilkka Lindblom

JacqueLyn Lobelle

Vicky London

Clare Lowe

Jean-Paul Lowe

Liz Lowry

Elizabeth Lubowitz

Felix Lundström

Pamela Luse

Anna Lyaruu

Anthony Lynch

Maxwell Patrick Lynch

The Macaulay-Brooks

Dan Mackie

Jo MacKinnon

Katie Maddock

David Mader

Laura Magnier

Erin Maher

Bonnie Maize

Kizzy Makinde-Corrick

Erik Malinowski

Michelle Mallett

Aaron Malone

Philippa Manasseh

Shubhang Mani

Amy Elizabeth Manlapas

Lea Mara

Catherine Mardula

Sarah Marrs

Amy Martin

Andreas Martin

Barbara Martin

Ellen Martin

Rory Martin

Angel Martinez

Dominic Mather

John Matthews

Andrew Matthias

Dave McAllister

Nancy McAllister

Kieran McCallum

Callum McCaul

Yvonne Carol McCombie

Jon McCorkell

Therese McCormick

Sarah McCullough

Teresa McDonold

Melissa McDowell

John A C McGowan

David McGuigan

Brittany McIntyre

Prue McKay

Haley McLoughlin

Leanna McPherson

Jarlath McQuaid

Laura McVey

Caren Meaney

Nina Mega

Carole Melia

Brian Mendonca

Kilian Metcalf

Josh Metivier

Deborah Metters

Anthony Micari

Roger Miles

Brian Millar

Ashley Miller

Jeffrey Mills

Justin Mingo

Wade Minter

Laurie J Mintz

Kathryn Mitchell

Mark Mitchell

John Mitchinson

Lucy Moffatt

Olly Mogs

Matthew Mole

Mike Monaco

Alastair Monk

Mariana Montes

Henry Monti

Tom Moody-Stuart

Kristoffer Moore

Andy Moran

C. Moretti

Bria Morgan

Daniel Morgan

Gareth Morgan

Matt Morgan

Paul Morgan

Ian Morrison

Micah Morrison

Elizabeth Morrissey

Barbara Mosley

Victoria Mosley

Carl Moss

motherofthedollgirl

Andrew Mueller

Robin Mulvihill

Mark Murphy

Muireann Murphy

Rachel Murphy

Mo Nassar

Carlo Navato

Nicholas Nelson

Samuel Nelson

Zak Nesvitsky

Brad Newman

Daisy Newstead

Roo Newton

Lydy Nickerson

Orlando Nicoletti

Lasse Nielsen

Alexander Nirenberg

Benedict Nolan

Simon Nott

Conrad Nowikow

Alex Nye

An Nyx-Dubhadh

Peter O'Brien

Paul O'Driscoll

Caoimhe O'Gorman

Elizabeth O'Hara

Quinn O'Hara-Brantner

Aidan O'Sullivan

Ciara O'Sullivan

Huw O'Sullivan

Karen O'Sullivan

Clare O'Neill

Oliver Ockenden

Heather Oldfield

Michael Orr

Justin Owen

Lynne Owen

Josh Owens

Craig Oxbrow

Cro Page

Evan Panagopoulos

Themistocles Papassilekas

Steph Parker

Sarah Marie Parker-Allen

Alan Parkinson

Gill Parrott & Nick Parfitt

Julie Parsons

Karen Passmore

James Paterson

Trish Paton

Sue Patrick

Sally Patterson

Sally Paustian

Andy Pavis

Michelle Pawlak

Matthew Pearce

Robert Pence

Craig Penrose

Richard Percy

Bruce Perry

Claire Perry

Elizabeth Perry

David Peters

Nathaniel Peters

Kylee Peterson

Zachary Peterson

Timothy J Petro

Charity A. Petrov

Christophe Pettus

Jonathan Phillips

Tom Phillips

Jenny Pichierri

Justin Pickard

Eric Platt

Suzy Plows

Lucy Plunkett

Athena Pogue

Justin Pollard

Eric Pollock

Thomas Ponton

Sam Pred

Janet Pretty

Lawrence Pretty

David Prew

Alison Price

Claire Price

Rhian Heulwen Price

Caroline Pulver

Anna Puma

Cecilia Quirk

Janel Quoc

James Raasch

Michael Rader

Liza Radley

Sean Raffey

Todd Ramsey

Natasha Ranken

Anne Rantanen

Bast Ravenshadow

Janet Rawlings

James Redstone

Nora Reed

Barry Rees

Mike "Spicy Mike" Reeves

Corinne Reimers

Ian S. Reinard

Claire Rendell

Electra Rhodes

Thomas Ribbits

Robert Ritchie

Deb Roberts

Lisa Roberts

Richard Roberts

Wyn Roberts

Anthea Robertson

Louis Robertson

Kenn Roessler

Wojciech Rogoziński

Gregory Rosmaita

Acoustic Ross

Jennifer Ross

Laura Rothwell

Georgie Rowe

Catherine Rowlands

Stephen Rowley

Brian Rudin

V J Ruggiero

Bonnie Russell

Merc Rustad

Alex Rutherford

Andrew Ryan

Donna Ryan

Jack Ryder

Amanda S

Dana Saeger

Teraza Salmon

Erin Salter

Zannah Salter

Gabriele Sanchez

Thomas F Santarelli

Lucy Saunders

Shrikant Sawant

Ericka Schenck

Arthur Schiller

Garrett Schneider

Vlad Schüler Costa

Nicole Schulman

Amber Scott

Jonathan Scott

Lesley Scott

Rebecca Seibel

Dick Selwood

Joe Selzer

Cathleen Sessions

Belynda J. Shadoan

Shawntay Shannon

Sam Sharp

Caitlyn Shauger

Kristal Sheets

Shepherd

Keith Sherratt

Hannah Shipman

James Shirbin

Erik Shirokoff

Jonathan Short

Matt Sias

Alex Silloway

Yalina Silva

Adam Simmons

Emma Simmons

Ann Simon

Alan Sims

Jill Singer

Danielle Skjelver

Robert Slaymaker

Keith Sleight

Russell Smeaton

Adrian Smith

Andrew Smith

Billy Smith

Brian Smith

Jane Smith

Joel Smith

Karl Smith

Kate Smith

Matt Smith

Megan Smith

Michael Smith

Nicola Smithson

Sara C. Snider

L Snijder

Elizabeth Soellner

Linda Sohl

Judith Solberg

Soror Somnia Clare

Michael Sorgatz

Steve Southart

Kerri J Spangaro

Frank Spring

Caroline Springer

R J Squirrel

Marc St-Laurent

Gimond St.Paulios

Mark Stalzer

Ginger Stampley

Paul Stanley

Greg Stedman

Julian C. Steen

Mark Steenbakkers

Sterling Stein

David Stelling

G Stephen

Lindy Stephens

Ros Stern

Steven Steven

Kyle Stevens

Vicki Stevens

Elizabeth Stewart

Lisa Stockholm

Katie Straker

Rae Streets

Tim Striplin

Eric Stroshane

James Stuart

Shawn Stuart

Nina Stutler

Cindy Syes

Ian Synge

Nulani t'Acraya

Laine Taffin Altman

Tracey Taggart

Jean Takabayashi

Sarah Talks

Toni Tallon

Emma Tanner

Bruce Tarkington

William Tatum

Alex Taylor

Bethany Taylor

Georgette Taylor

Samantha Taylor

Jami Taylor Parylak

Nicole Teixeira

Holly Thackeray

Steven Thomas

Leivur Thomassen

Christine Thompson

David Thompson

Jo Thompson

Patrick Thomson

Julie Thorfinnson

Richard Thorpe

Robert Tienken

Simon Tierney-Wigg

Jamie Tobutt

Rosanna Tolle and John Tolle

Lorna Toolis

Mitch Trale

Jonathan Travaglia

Julia Trocme-Latter

Brett Trotter-King

Brian Trowbridge

Stefanie Tryson

David G Tubby

Richard Tubman

Steve Tuckwell

Harry Tuffs

Edward Tumber

James Tunnicliffe

Abby Turner

Dr. Cathy Ullman

Karen Unland

Amandeep Kaur Uppal

Rob Vance

Brian Vander Veen

Mark Vent

Andréa W

Elizabeth Wadsworth

Brock Wager

Judy Walker

Meghan Walker

Joe Walkowski

Susan Wall

Andrew Walsh

Kim Walsh

Karen Walton

Philip Ward

Neil Warner

Camille Warren

Katherine Warry

Stephanie Wasek

Andrew Weaver

Callum Weaver

Julie Weber-Roark

Sebastian Wegener

John Wellings

Alexandra Welsby

Kristin Westphal

Samuel Westwood

Deanna Westwood MA

Charles Wheeler

Doreen Wheeler

Tarah Wheeler

Teresa Whitaker

Georgina White

Rebecca White

Andrew Whitwham

Diana Whyland Packard

David Widdick

Jack Wilkes

Annette Wilkinson

Arnold Williams

Jenny Williams

Jo Williams

Jonathan Williams

Kate Williams

Neil Williams

Tony Williamson

Zoë-Elise Williamson

Hanna Williamson-Sparks

Alice Willison

Dan Wilson

Gavin Wilson

Natalie Wilson

Stephen Wilson

Janey Winterbauer

Robyn Winters

Alice Wiseman

Puzzle Wizard

Anton Wolf

Mischa Wolfinger

Thomas Wolfskeller

Lesley Wood

James Woodcock

Mark Woodward

Wendalynn Wordsmith

Douglas M Worth

Steve Wren

Dr Stuart Wright

Mark Wright

Emily Wros

Debbie Wythe

Christie Yant

Owen Yapp

Nate Young

Anthony Zacharzewski

Marcus Zachrisson

Brenda Zary-Jones

Rui Zhong

Clayton Zink